MW01132642

The Coming Kingdom of Christ

By John R. Rice, D.D., Litt.D.

Author of *Prayer—Asking and Receiving*; *The Home: Courtship, Marriage and Children*; *Twelve Tremendous Themes*; *The Ruin of a Christian*; *Revival Appeals, etc.* Editor of THE SWORD OF THE LORD

A Bible study on the return of Christ, the coming restoration and conversion of Israel, the re-establishment of David's throne at Jerusalem, Christ's reign thereon for a thousand years, and the eternal Heaven upon the earth where all the saints of God of all ages will dwell in eternal rapture in the presence of our Father, God, and His dear Son, our Saviour, Jesus Christ.

SWORD OF THE LORD PUBLISHERS
MURFREESBORO, TENNESSEE

11,500 copies previously printed
5,000 copies, October, 1948
5,000 copies, February, 1954
2,000 copies, January, 1966
2,000 copies, October, 1968
2,000 copies, July, 1971
2,500 copies, September, 1973
2,500 copies, January, 1976
1,500 copies, August, 1979

ISBN 0-87398-116-2

Preface

"Thy kingdom come. Thy will be done in earth, as it is in heaven."—Matt. 6:10

ITH MINGLED joy and anxiety I present this book to Christian readers everywhere. I am anxious because the matters taught are so weighty. I earnestly pray that God will make the truths that are herein presented clear to every humble heart who willingly seeks to know what God has promised and the things that "must shortly come to pass." But there is a great joy in the telling of this story. My own heart has been so blessed in the long months of preparation, study, prayer, and writing, that I cannot but feel that others likewise will be blessed.

The burden of the book is this: that Christ will return to this earth, restore Israel to Palestine and save them, and will establish again the throne of David, and from that throne rule over the entire earth; that this kingdom will be a literal kingdom of a visible Christ reigning over a literal people; that eventually Heaven will be on this earth. Many other details of teaching will become clear as you read. All I ask is that you give to the reading an open mind and a prayerful, humble heart, and that you search the Scriptures to see whether these things are so.

Two things particularly characterize this volume. The first is that nearly one line in three of the book is actual Scripture quotations. Many, many other Scripture references are given. The whole matter must be settled by the Word of God. It is a book of Bible teaching. I trust and earnestly believe that this feature will make the book valuable to the well-versed Bible scholar and at the same time understandable and rich to the beginning student who knows little of the Word of God.

The other outstanding characteristic is that the Scriptures are taken at face value. I believe the Bible. I believe it says what it means. I believe that humble, prayerful hearts who approach the Word of God in reverent faith will find its treasures fully available, and each one may fill his vessel to the full. Worldly wisdom is not sufficient, for God has hidden these things from the wise and prudent and revealed them unto babes. So we take the Scriptures at face value. "Israel" means Israel. "Jerusalem" means Jerusalem. "For ever" means forever. "A thousand years" means a thousand years. All the promises of God are "yea and amen." If Abraham, Isaac, Jacob, Moses, David, and the apostles believed the promises about the coming kingdom, then we may safely do the same.

Some say the promised reign of Christ on the throne of David will never come to pass. Others say it began during His earthly ministry. Still others believe that at Pentecost the kingdom was set up and that the church and kingdom are the same. Still others believe that the Scriptural promises and prophecies on these matters are highly figurative, cannot be understood, and that we should leave the study of unfulfilled prophecies and preach only those that have been fulfilled. But the careful and prayerful reader who checks this little book by THE Book will learn that God has promised a kingdom on this earth when the Lord Jesus Himself shall reign gloriously in Jerusalem over all the earth.

Please do not be offended at the positive ring throughout the book. Before you are through you will see, I trust, that this book presents only the clear, positive teachings of the Word of God. If we were guessing about dates, or speculating on things not revealed, we might well be more timid. There is much about the future that we do not know. Many faithful and good teachers and preachers of the Bible do not agree about details. But the great body of truth concerning the fact of Christ's literal return and literal reign on this earth are so clearly taught that for a humble and open-minded believer to know what God's Word says on these matters is simply to accept it and be glad.

For myself it was so. Reared and trained altogether under the teachings of postmillennialists in Sunday School, preaching service, college, university, and seminary, when I began the independent study of my Bible I was compelled and then happy to accept this Bible teaching.

In closing, may I say that the purpose of the book is not only to make clear a great Bible teaching but to establish a Hope and show Christians that it is the blessed Hope. I earnestly pray that hearts will be blessed even more than heads.

To me it is surprisingly sweet to know that there is coming a day when the kingdoms of this world shall become the kingdoms

of our Lord and of His Christ; when the pure in heart shall see
God, and when the meek shall inherit the earth; when the eyes of
the blind shall be opened, and the ears of the deaf shall be unstopped, when the lame shall leap as an hart, and the tongue of
the dumb shall sing, and when sorrow and sighing shall flee away.
Our arms will hold again our dear ones, loved and lost awhile,
and we shall see Him whom we love because He first loved us.
I trust that the longing in your heart, as you read this book, will
teach you to pray sincerely in the words the Saviour taught us,
"Thy kingdom come. Thy will be done in earth, as it is in
heaven" (Matt. 6:10), and like the beloved John, "Even so, come,
Lord Jesus"! (Rev. 22:20).

I take this occasion to acknowledge my debt to many who have
helped to make this book possible. The writings of Dr. R. A. Tor-
rey, Dr. C. I. Scofield, Dr. W. E. Blackstone and many others have
taught me to take heed to the "more sure word of prophecy" "as
unto a light that shineth in a dark place." I owe to the ministry
of such men a debt of gratitude which words can only poorly
express.

The defects of the book must be many. My heart cries out that
however much of prayer and study and labor has been bestowed
upon the book I am an unprofitable servant. Yet before now God
has chosen the foolish things of the world to confound the
mighty, and He who blessed Moses' rod and Gideon's lamp, and
the jawbone in the hand of Samson, can surely bless this. I put it
in His hands as the little boy put the loaves and fishes there for
Him to multiply and feed the hungry multitude. May He get
glory to His great name! Hallelujah! What a Saviour!

". . . and the government shall be upon his shoulder: . . . Of the increase of his government and peace there shall be no end, upon the throne of David, and upon his kingdom, to order it, and to establish it with judgment and with justice from henceforth even for ever."—Isa. 9:6, 7.

"And the Lord shall be king over all the earth." —Zech. 14:9.

"Thy kingdom come. Thy will be done in earth, as it is in heaven."—Matt. 6:10.

". . . and the Lord God shall give unto him the throne of his father David: And He shall reign over the house of Jacob for ever; and of his kingdom there shall be no end."—Luke 1:32, 33.

"Behold, he cometh with clouds; and every eye shall see him, and they also which pierced him: and all kindreds of the earth shall wail because of him. Even so, Amen."—Rev. 1:7.

". . . and we shall reign on the earth."—Rev. 5:10.

"Amen. Even so, come, Lord Jesus."—Rev. 22:20.

Table of Contents

Chapter 1

Blessings in the Study of Prophecy

CHRISTIAN people are constantly confronted by certain great questions. People are hungry to have the facts about such questions as these:

1. Why did all the Jews expect Christ to have a literal kingdom on earth? David understood that some great Descendant would continue his kingdom on this earth permanently. The Jews in the time of Christ expected some great Son of David to arise and establish again the Jewish monarchy. The wise men came to find "the King of the Jews," and even Herod was alarmed because he expected a King to be born who would restore David's kingdom over Israel. Even the apostles, and that after the resurrection of Jesus, were looking for the restoration of the kingdom to Israel (Acts 1:6). WHY? Had God given them reason to expect a literal kingdom on earth?

2. Will this war-torn world ever have real, permanent, world-wide peace? Men's efforts have failed. Peace treaties have become weapons of offense. All the world's culture, civilization, and science have only succeeded in making war more terrible, more heartless, more bloody. Will this war-torn world ever have peace? If so, when, and how?

3. Will the curse placed on this world because of sin ever be removed so that man can live here in a new Garden of Eden? Weeds still grow easier than corn. Science only slightly modifies the terrible scourge of insect pests. Disease increases. Drought, floods, earthquakes and tornadoes ravage the earth. This whole planet groans and travails because of sin. Will man ever subdue this earth and have dominion over it as God commanded, as Adam lived in Eden at perfect peace with all animal life and the elements of nature?

4. Has the glory of Israel departed forever? Has God cast away forever the nation of Abraham, Isaac, Jacob, David and the apostles? Or will God yet restore the nation Israel to its own land, Canaan, united, happy, and saved?

5. Christians talk much of Heaven; where will Heaven be through eternity? Will it be in some mystic, uncertain, far-off state where spirits without bodies gather, or will it be the paradise of God set up on this earth?

These Questions Answered in the Bible

The Bible answers these questions, definitely, explicitly, in chapter after chapter and verse after verse. Surprising as it may seem, every preacher who knows his Bible can show you the answer to any one of these five questions, with dozens of Scriptures to prove it in the Word of God. The Bible answers these questions so clearly that they never would have been asked but for the ignorance of those who do not know the Bible and the folly of those who explain away the plain, literal teachings of God's Word.

The simple fact is, that people generally know nothing about the prophetic portions of the Bible. The denominational seminaries usually do not attempt to teach these portions. The average pastor never preaches on prophecy, thinks it of no special importance and admits that he does not understand it. And many people foolishly call a discussion of prophecy "speculation." Many Bible teachers and preachers say that these prophecies are so highly figurative that they cannot be understood and that perhaps most of them have already been fulfilled in a figurative sense. The International Sunday School lesson committee deliberately avoids these prophecies. Satan has evidently set out to keep from the people a knowledge of what God has plainly foretold will come to pass.

"There Shall Come in the Last Days Scoffers"

The Bible plainly foretells this attitude of skepticism toward prophecy and particularly toward the return of Christ in II Peter 3:3-5, as follows:

"Knowing this first, that there shall come in the last days scoffers, walking after their own lusts, And saying, Where is the promise of his coming? for since the fathers fell asleep, all things

continue as they were from the beginning of the creation. For this they willingly are ignorant of, that by the word of God the heavens were of old, and the earth standing out of the water and in the water."

Notice that these scoffers about the second coming of Christ are worldly in their living, "walking after their own lusts," and are modernistic in their doctrine; that is, they "willingly are ignorant" of the direct creation of the world by the Word of God. Evidently this Scripture has come to pass, is being fulfilled before our eyes. It is a pitiful fact that in these modern days Christians, and often preachers, walk after their own lusts and have the same habits, companions and entertainments as the unsaved world. This Scripture has also come to pass in these last days, that men, even so-called Christian college and seminary teachers, and some preachers "willingly are ignorant" of the fact "that by the word of God the heavens were of old, and the earth standing out of the water and in the water." People willingly remain ignorant of the direct creation of the world as given in Genesis, and instead of that substitute the modern doctrine of evolution.

But, says the Scripture above, given us by inspiration through the Apostle Peter, the outstanding characteristic about these men who will appear in the last days is that they are scoffers, casting doubt about the second coming of Christ, saying, "Where is the promise of his coming? for since the fathers fell asleep, all things continue as they were from the beginning of the creation." How many, many preachers are scoffers about the prophecies of the future so plainly given and so often repeated in the Bible! The Devil has raised up these scoffers among Bible teachers and preachers, Sunday School lesson writers, and seminaries, to keep the masses of the people ignorant concerning God's plain statements of the things which must come to pass.

It is fair to say that many good, earnest men who love the Lord and believe the Bible have been mistaught and are ignorant concerning the great prophecies of the Bible. Many a preacher preaches all the truth he knows, but has been discouraged in the study of prophecy by better scholars than he. Then there have been many charlatans and false teachers who have brought reproach on the prophetic portions of God's Word. Many people very foolishly set dates for the second coming of Christ, when Jesus plainly said that no man knows the day nor the hour, and that all should watch for that time which would come as suddenly as a thief in the night. Seventh Day Adventists, Millerites, Jehovah's Witnesses, Anglo-Israel teachers and many others have brought discredit on prophetic teaching. But how foolish it is to neglect and ignore half of the Bible because it has been mistaught by others! The prophetic portion of the Bible is still God's Word and is intended to be read, to be taught, and to be understood.

More Than Half of Bible Prophecies Not Yet Fulfilled!

Most people do not realize how much of the future is told in the Bible. They know that many things about Christ's first coming, His birth, His sufferings, His death and resurrection are foretold in the Old Testament. They do not know that hundreds of details concerning the resurrection of the Christian dead, the changing of the bodies of living Christians, our marriage to Christ and our honeymoon, a great tribulation on this earth, the rise of the Antichrist (a world dictator), the last great battle on earth, the setting up of the kingdom of Christ, the regathering of Israel to one land, their conversion, the restoration of the kingdom of David, the final doom of Satan, judgment of sinners, and the moving of God the Father and His house of many mansions to the new earth for the remainder of eternity, are told with fascinating clearness!

Far more than half of the prophecies of the Bible are as yet unfulfilled. The prophecies which have not been fulfilled are as definite, as literal, and as easily understood as the prophecies which have been fulfilled already. The second coming of Christ is foretold as clearly as is the first coming, and the incidents connected with it are as clear as it was that He should be born at Bethlehem, that He should be of the tribe of Judah, descended from David, born of a virgin, that He should enter Jerusalem on an ass and that He should preach the gospel to the poor. Those were literal happenings, literally foretold. The literal facts about His crucifixion, including the gamble for His garments, the very words of the priests before the cross, the piercing of His hands and feet, and the cry of Jesus, "My God, my God, why hast thou forsaken me?" all were so literally foretold that the most brazen skeptic could not deny their fulfillment. We have no reason to believe that the remainder of the prophecies will be fulfilled a̱ less literally than these. Oftentimes the prophecies about the sec ond coming of Jesus are in the same chapters or same verses with these other prophecies which have been already fulfilled, definitely and literally.

Unfulfilled Prophecies Can Be Understood

Sometimes people who do not know much about prophecies, or who do not believe they will be literally fulfilled, excuse themselves by saying that one cannot understand a prophecy until it has been fulfilled and that therefore we should not study nor try to interpret unfulfilled prophecies. A brief reflection ought to convince anybody that that is not true. Prophecies are given ahead of time so that people may be warned. They can be understood, and that is exactly the reason they are given.

For example, Noah prepared for the flood, built an ark, and preached to the wicked generation before the flood; and all Noah knew about it he got from prophecies that were not yet fulfilled! He did not ignore those prophecies nor think they might be figurative, but he knew what would happen and what he should do in preparation.

Lot in Sodom, and Abraham outside of Sodom, knew ahead of time that the wicked city, with others, would be destroyed by the wrath of God. All they knew about it was from the Lord's prophecies that had not yet been fulfilled. But that is what prophecies are for, so we may be prepared when the things come to pass.

The Flood and the Destruction of Sodom, Like the Return of Christ

The judgment of God on the whole earth in the flood, and on Sodom and Gomorrah in the days of Lot, are mentioned by the Saviour in Matthew 24:37–42 and Luke 17:26–30 as typical of the events surrounding the coming of the Saviour. Jesus said, "But as the days of Noe were, so shall also the coming of the Son of man be." Those prophecies of the future were given to be understood ahead of time, and so are the prophecies of the Bible which are yet unfulfilled.

I remind you that just as we do not know the time of the Saviour's coming, so the exact time of the flood and of the de-

struction of Sodom and Gomorrah by fire and brimstone from the
Lord out of Heaven were not foretold. But the essential facts
were foretold plainly and the prophecies were fulfilled literally.
So we may expect it to be with the prophecies which have not yet
been fulfilled.

It is a fact, then, that unfulfilled prophecies can be understood.
We are not to go beyond what the Bible says. We are not to teach
guesses nor speculation nor what we imagine about the future,
but what the Lord has revealed. And that we may take at face
value, believing that it will be fulfilled to the letter, and literally,
as were the prophecies which have been fulfilled heretofore.

Practically all we know about Heaven, about Hell, about the
resurrection of our bodies, about rewards and judgments, we
know from unfulfilled prophecies.

Many Prophecies of Christ's First Coming Were Understood Before Time

The Old Testament is full of references to Jesus. Jesus is the
theme of all the Bible, the Old as well as the New. Jesus said,
"Moses . . . wrote of me"; He said, "Abraham rejoiced to see my
day: and he saw it, and was glad." Peter preached to Cornelius
that "To him give all the prophets witness, that through his name
whosover believeth in him shall receive remission of sins" (Acts
10:43). How foolish it would be to have the Old Testament full
of predictions of prophecies about the first coming of the Saviour
if none of them could be understood ahead of time.

The fact is that many, many of these prophecies were understood ahead of time. The wicked scribes and Pharisees knew and
told Herod that the Saviour was to be born in Bethlehem (Matt.
2:3–6). They knew that Christ should live forever (John 12:34).
The more spiritually-minded seemed to have known (probably
from Daniel 9:24, 25) the time of His birth. Remember the wise
men (Matt. 2:1, 2), and Simeon (Luke 2:26). Even the common
people seemed to be expecting Jesus when He began His ministry
(John 7:31). Christ's virgin birth (Isaiah 7:14), His descent from
David (Jer. 23:5, 6), His birth at Bethlehem (Micah 5:2), were so
thoroughly made known in prophecies, before they were fulfilled,
that all might have known they would literally come to pass, and
many did know. The time of the Second Coming is not foretold,

but Daniel 9:25 told ahead of time that the first coming of Christ would be sixty-nine sevens of years (483 years) after the command to restore Jerusalem and the temple in the days of Nehemiah and Ezra!

It is silly to say that unfulfilled prophecies cannot be understood. That is what they are given for, to be understood. Of course, there are depths to the prophecies and to all Scripture that human beings have not yet fathomed. When I read John 3:16, I cannot know all about how much God loved me! But thank God, I can clearly understand that He did love me and that He gave Christ to die for me, and that by believing on Him I have everlasting life. Unfulfilled prophecies, then, are to be read, studied, and taught like other parts of the Bible.

Special Blessing Promised in the Study of the Prophecies

The Lord promised special blessings to those who read, who hear, and who understand prophecies. In Matthew 13:10–17, Jesus stated this principle, that since His coming many things not understood by the prophets and righteous men of old are now revealed, but only to spiritually-minded people. He did not explain the parables of the kingdom of Heaven to the public, but did to His disciples, saying in Matthew 13:16–17:

"But blessed are your eyes, for they see: and your ears, for they hear. For verily I say unto you, That many prophets and righteous men have desired to see those things which ye see, and have not seen them; and to hear those things which ye hear, and have not heard them."

Jesus has a special blessing for those whose hearts are humble and attentive to His teaching about prophecies.

Likewise in Revelation 1:3, the same Lord Jesus, in giving John the book of Revelation, said, "Blessed is he that readeth, and they that hear the words of this prophecy, and keep those things which are written therein: for the time is at hand." Remember that the book of Revelation has a divinely inspired title given in the first verse, "The Revelation of Jesus Christ." The subject of the book of Revelation is the course of events culminating in the public revelation of Jesus Christ visibly to the whole world. And the Lord Jesus promised a special blessing to those

who read, hear and keep the things written in this prophecy!
Prophecy can be understood. Christians not only can understand
the prophecies but are plainly commanded to read and hear
them. So we should search the Bible for answers to our questions.

Unfulfilled Prophecy "a Light That Shineth in a Dark Place"

Not only can unfulfilled prophecies be understood, but they
are the only lights we have in this dark world as concerns the future. Science can give no assurance about what will happen tomorrow. The rulers of the nations who in some sense have in their
care the lives of millions, can only grope in an ever increasing
darkness, wondering what tomorrow will bring. But the Scriptures, thank God, will tell us; and God's prophetic Word shines
on the future as light in a dark place. So says the Word of God.
Second Peter 1:19 says: "We have also a more sure word of prophecy; whereunto ye do well that ye take heed, as unto a light that
shineth in a dark place, until the day dawn, and the day star arise
in your hearts." Prophecy of the future is "sure." It is not speculation nor guess but sure revelation. To this prophecy yet unfulfilled, "ye do well that ye take heed," as the only dependable light
in the dark, and keep on heeding "until the day dawn"! We are
commanded to take heed to prophecy. There is a special blessing
on those who study prophecy. Unfulfilled prophecy is a light shining in a dark place. Christians who know and understand the
prophecies of the Bible will walk in the light and not in darkness,
knowing the "things which must shortly come to pass."

Why Jews Expected Christ to Set Up a Literal, Earthly Kingdom

We do not have to seek far to learn why the Jews of the time of
Christ, even including the apostles, all expected Jesus to set up a
literal kingdom on the earth. The reason is that the Bible plainly
and repeatedly, from one end to the other, teaches that He will do
exactly that. It tells that the kingdom will be over Jews. It tells
many times that that kingdom will be centered in the land of
Canaan or Palestine. The Bible repeats many times that the King
will be a Descendant of David and will rule in the place of David,
from the same place, that is, from the same throne. The Bible
likewise makes clear that that kingdom will be a literal kingdom
on a literal throne over a literal land.

Now, if your mind has been stirred enough to investigate honestly this matter, blessed are you! If so, you are getting ready to enjoy your Bible as you never did before and to learn things that you never dreamed were in the Word of God. May God bless you and help you to learn for yourself some of the mysterious and wonderful things God has foretold as certain to come to pass. Let us learn, then, about God's promises to Abraham, to David, to the children of Israel, to the eternal city Jerusalem, to the apostles, and to all Christians.

Chapter 2

God's Covenant With Abraham: His Seed to Possess Canaan Forever

ONE OF THE earliest great promises which has not yet been fulfilled is the promise that the people Israel is to possess the land of Canaan for an everlasting possession.

In Genesis 12:1–3 we are told that Abraham was called out from his country in Ur of the Chaldees, away from his kinspeople and relatives, to a land that the Lord would show him, the land of Canaan. With that call, God had given Abraham this great promise in Genesis 12:2, 3:

"And I will make of thee a great nation, and I will bless thee, and make thy name great; and thou shalt be a blessing: And I will bless them that bless thee, and curse him that curseth thee: and in thee shall all families of the earth be blessed."

God there selected Abraham and his descendants to form a great nation through which He would bless the world. All the Bible, except the first eleven chapters, reminds us again and again that the nation Israel has been called and selected of God to be a blessing to the whole world.

After God called Abraham to the land of Canaan, the land itself was given to Abraham. That in itself would not seem so remarkable, but with the gift went an everlasting promise that all the land would be given, not only to Abraham, but TO HIS SEED FOREVER! Read Genesis 13:14, 15 which says:

"And the Lord said unto Abram, after that Lot was separated from him, Lift up now thine eyes, and look from the place where thou art northward, and southward, and eastward, and westward:

God's Covenant With Abraham

For all the land which thou seest, to thee will I give it, and to thy seed for ever."

The land of Palestine has been given unconditionally to Israelites, to Abraham and the descendants of Abraham, for an everlasting possession. In fact, that term "an everlasting possession" is exactly what God said to Abraham when He mentioned the matter again in Genesis 17:8: "And I will give unto thee, and to thy seed after thee, the land wherein thou art a stranger, all the land of Canaan, for an everlasting possession; and I will be their God." Did you notice in reading the above verse that God said "all the land of Canaan"? It is the literal land, Canaan, which was promised to Abraham. It is ALL of the land of Canaan, also. Its proper boundaries are mentioned in the first of Joshua. Now only a comparatively few Jews are in the land of Canaan, and they certainly do not possess it, own it, and rule over it, as was promised.

The Promise Must Be Fulfilled to Abraham in Person

In both the Scriptures mentioned above, the land of Canaan is promised to Abraham himself, in person, as well as to his descendants. Genesis 13:15 says, "TO THEE will I give it, and to thy seed for ever." Genesis 17:8 says, "And I will give UNTO THEE, and to thy seed after thee, the land wherein thou art a stranger, all the land of Canaan, for an everlasting possession." The promise is not just that some day the descendants of Abraham would take possession of the land of Canaan, but that he himself would be present and in possession.

Jews in past generations have possessed the land of Canaan. In Joshua 21:43–45 we are told how Israelites under Joshua possessed the land.

"And the Lord gave unto Israel all the land which he sware to give unto their fathers; and they possessed it, and dwelt therein. And the Lord gave them rest round about, according to all that he sware unto their fathers: and there stood not a man of all their enemies before them; the Lord delivered all their enemies into their hand. There failed not ought of any good thing which the Lord had spoken unto the house of Israel; all came to pass."

There are at least two important things in the promise to Abraham which were not fulfilled when the nation Israel took possession of the land of Canaan. One thing is that Abraham himself did not have possession. The promise was primarily to him. He never had before that time and did not then possess the land. God did not say to Abraham, "Unto thee THROUGH thy seed I will give the land." But He did say, "Unto thee AND to thy seed." That was not fulfilled when Israel took the land under Joshua's leadership.

Another part of the promise clearly was not fulfilled. That is, the possession was to be eternal. It was to be "an everlasting possession." That was not fulfilled when the nation Israel conquered the land of Canaan. Individuals died and did not possess it forever, and eventually the whole nation was scattered and lost national possession of the land. The covenant to Abraham was not fulfilled at that time.

Read Joshua 21:43 again carefully. That verse plainly indicates that the covenant was not fulfilled. The Lord simply gave unto Israel, "the land which he sware to give UNTO THEIR FATHERS." Joshua 21:45 says: "There failed not ought of any good thing which the Lord had spoken unto the house of Israel; all came to pass." Does that mean that God had fulfilled all He had promised ever to do for Israel? Does it mean that the kingdom of David, foretold in Deuteronomy 17:14–20, had been fulfilled? Certainly not. Did it mean that the promise of the Saviour, which promise was given particularly to that nation in Deuteronomy 18:15, had been fulfilled? Certainly not. Did it mean that a *TEMPORARY* possession of the land of Canaan by Jews of that generation fulfilled the promise of *ETERNAL* possession by Abraham and his seed? CERTAINLY NOT! Joshua 21:45 simply states that God had kept all His promises up to date, having done at that time and to that people all that He had promised to do at that time to that people. None of God's promises had failed.

And if God's promises up to that date had not failed, and if His promises to us up to date have not failed, can we not surely expect that of His promises to Abraham and his seed not one good thing shall fail? God keeps His promises!

The promise about eternal possession of the land was to Abraham in person as well as his seed, and when it is fulfilled the possession will continue forever.

How Long Does "For Ever" Mean?

The Bible ought to be taken at face value. God's Word means what it says. God promised Abraham "for all the land which thou seest, to thee will I give it, and to thy seed FOR EVER." Again He promised Abraham "all the land of Canaan, for an EVERLASTING possession." The only honest and safe way to interpret these statements is not to interpret them at all but simply take them at face value. The word "for ever" means forever. The word "everlasting" means everlasting. Do not explain away the Scriptures.

The Hebrew word *olam* translated "for ever" in Genesis 13:15 is the same word translated "for ever" in II Samuel 7:26 when David said "let thy name be magnified for ever." It is the same word translated "for ever" in Psalms 66:7, "He ruleth by his power for ever." If God's name would be magnified forever, and if He is to rule by His power forever, then Abraham, in person, and his seed are to possess the land of Caanan forever. Many other examples could be given showing that it means in the original Hebrew just what it is translated to mean in English. "For ever" means forever, and that is how long Abraham and his seed are to inhabit Canaan!

God's Promise to Abraham Is Yet to Be Fulfilled

In the above promises, God said to Abraham about the land of Canaan, "To thee WILL I give it, and to thy seed for ever" (Gen. 13:15), and again in Genesis 17:8, the Lord said, "I WILL give unto thee, and to thy seed. . . ." Notice that in each case the Lord used the future tense, "I will." The promises are for the future. Abraham never expected in his first and natural life on this earth to possess all the land of Canaan. Hebrews 11:8 makes clear that Abraham was not promised *IMMEDIATE* possession of the land, but was called to a land which he should *AFTERWARDS* inherit. With this in mind, read carefully Hebrews 11:8–13 as follows:

"By faith Abraham, when he was called to go out into a place which he SHOULD AFTER RECEIVE FOR AN INHERITANCE, obeyed; and he went out, not knowing whither he went. By faith he sojourned in THE LAND OF PROMISE, as in a strange country, dwelling in tabernacles with Isaac and Jacob, the HEIRS with him of the same promise: For he looked for a city which hath foundations, whose builder and maker is God. Through faith also Sara herself received strength to conceive seed, and was delivered of a child when she was past age, because she judged him faithful who had promised. Therefore sprang there even of one, and him as good as dead, so many as the stars of the sky in multitude, and as the sand which is by the sea shore innumerable. THESE ALL DIED IN FAITH, NOT HAVING RECEIVED THE PROMISES, but having seen them afar off, and were persuaded of them, and embraced them, and confessed that they were strangers and pilgrims on the earth."

—Heb. 11:8–13.

Abraham, Isaac and Jacob, with Sarah, were sojourners in the land which God had promised to give them in the future, but which they had not yet received. Later all of the Jewish nation, who by faith became heirs of the same promise, "As the sand which is by the sea shore innumerable," verse 13 tells us, died in faith, not having received the promises but having embraced them by faith. Evidently all the saved Israelites down to the time the book of Hebrews was written were heirs of this promise, but had not received it. Down to the time of Christ, then, the promises to Abraham, that the land of Canaan should be given to him and his children for an everlasting possession, had not been fulfilled! The promise that Israel is to possess the land of Canaan forever is yet in the future.

Stephen Said Abraham Had Not Yet Inherited Canaan

In that wonderful sermon by the Spirit-filled Stephen in Acts, chapter 7, we are told plainly that God called Abraham out of Mesopotamia, into the land of Canaan, but while Abraham lived there God did not let him inherit it as his own. In Acts 7:5 he says about Abraham: "And he gave him none inheritance in it, no, not so much as to set his foot on: yet he promised that he would give it to him for a possession, and to his seed after him, when **as** yet he had no child." Abraham did not inherit the land of Canaan, "not so much as to set his foot on." Let no one claim that promise to Abraham has been fulfilled, for it has not.

Literal, Physical Possession of Canaan Promised to Abraham and Christ Together

The passage above surely must have convinced you that the promise to Abraham of eternal possession of the land of Palestine has not yet been fulfilled. Abraham died, the Scripture says, "not having received the promises" (Heb. 11:13) having no inheritance in the land of Canaan as yet, "no, not so much as to set his foot on" (Acts 7:5). That physical inheritance of the land of Canaan by Abraham is future.

But here is another happy teaching of the Scripture in these same promises to Abraham. Christ Himself is to inherit, with Abraham, the physical land of Canaan. Genesis 13:15 says: "For all the land which thou seest, TO THEE will I give it, AND TO THY SEED for ever." Likewise Genesis 17:8 says: "And I will give unto THEE, and to THY SEED AFTER THEE, the land wherein thou art a stranger, all the land of Canaan, for an everlasting possession; and I will be their God."

Those promises concerning Abraham's seed are taken to mean the nation Israel, or at least those of Israel who by faith are the children of promise (Gen. 21:12; Gal. 3:29). God says, "I will be their God," so that indicates the plural seed of Abraham. Converted Israel will inherit Palestine with Abraham.

But Christ is Abraham's Seed, to whom the promises about inheriting Canaan were given with Abraham. Galatians 3:16 shows that God had in mind that Christ, Abraham's Seed, should inherit the land of Palestine forever with Abraham. "Now to Abraham and his seed were the promises made. He saith not, And to seeds, as of many; but as of one, And to thy seed, which is Christ." The New Testament adds further revelation to the Old. Abraham's seed does refer to Israel, but it certainly refers to Christ, we are here told. The promise to Abraham will be fulfilled and he will inherit the land. Likewise the promise to Christ will be fulfilled and He will inherit that land of Canaan. This proves two important facts. First, that Christ will have a literal reign on earth, and second, that this reign is future.

Christ Has Not Yet Inherited Canaan as a Possession

Abraham lived in the land of Canaan, but did not possess it. So Christ lived in the land of Canaan but did not possess it. Abraham was a stranger and a sojourner in the land of promise, but, we are told, did not inherit or come into actual possession of as much as to set foot upon (Acts 7:5). If that were true about Abraham with his riches in gold, silver, cattle, and servants (Gen. 13:2), it was even more true about Christ in His earthly life. Jesus was born and laid in a borrowed manger, crucified and laid in a borrowed grave. Between those events, He Himself told us that "the foxes have holes, and the birds of the air have nests; but the Son of man hath not where to lay his head" (Matt. 8:20). Jesus did not possess the land of Canaan for an inheritance.

The term "possession" used in the promises to Abraham is clearly defined by the circumstances when we are told that Abraham did not receive these promises during his lifetime. That proves it is a literal ownership and control, living on the land, which is promised to Abraham and so, physically, to Christ. What the promise meant about Abraham, it also means about Christ. If we cannot make the promise figurative with regard to Abraham, then it is not figurative about Christ. If Abraham was to have even more literal possession of the land than he had while here on earth before the promise was fulfilled, then Christ must have even more literal possession of the land than Abraham did before the promise to Him is fulfilled. It will not do, then, to explain away this Scripture and say that in some spiritual sense Christ in Heaven has already inherited Canaan. No, not until He has more literal control of it, and more literal possession of it than Abraham had, can Christ be said to have inherited the land of Canaan. The promise has not yet been fulfilled, but is for the future when Christ shall reign over the land of Canaan after His return to the earth.

In fact, if there is any land on this earth which Christ does not actually, literally possess, it is Palestine, and if there is any people on earth who have rejected Him as King, it is Abraham's seed, the Jews.

Surely your heart ought to be happy to realize that when Abraham comes back to possess the land promised to him as an everlasting possession, Christ will also possess that land.

God plainly told Abraham that his descendants would be carried down into Egypt for four hundred years (Gen. 15:13). The children of Israel later must have known that they would not at that time have an unbroken period of actual possession of the land of Canaan, since the Lord had plainly told them in Deuteronomy 28:63–68 that the nation would be scattered into all the world because of their sins. All of them understood and believed that.

Israelites to Live Forever on This Earth!

We have come to one great milestone of Bible teaching: the seed of Abraham, including Christ, are to possess and inhabit the land of Palestine forever. How many questions that answers! How many problems that settles! Where will Heaven be for Abraham? IT MUST INCLUDE PALESTINE ON THIS EARTH! Heaven, for Abraham and his believing descendants, at least, will include possessions on this earth.

Many other Scriptures throughout the Bible repeat God's promise to Israel about their land. For example, read the two following passages from Jeremiah:

"Then will I cause you to dwell in this place, in the land that I gave to your fathers, for ever and ever."—Jer. 7:7.
"They said, Turn ye again now every one from his evil way, and from the evil of your doings, and dwell in the land that the Lord hath given unto you and to your fathers for ever and ever."
—Jer. 25:5.

Not only did God give the land of Canaan to Abraham and his descendants, but He gave it to them "for ever and ever." The Bible by doubling the term makes the promise doubly sure. Jews are to live forever and ever on this earth in Palestine.

Actually, of course, if Heaven for Jews will be on earth, then Heaven for everybody will be on earth, as the Scripture makes plain later on. Here the promises are particularly to Abraham and his literal descendants. Saved Jews, children according to the promise, children of Abraham in both flesh and spirit, are to in-habit the land of Palestine forever in a Heaven on earth.

I was taught as a child in Sunday School that at the second coming of Christ there would be one general resurrection of all the dead, saved and unsaved. I was taught that this planet would be burned up and destroyed and disappear. I was taught that there would be at that time one general judgment and that saved and unsaved would alike stand before God to be judged according to their works. In some mysterious way it was supposed that Christ would intervene in behalf of the Christians. Then the un-saved would be sent to Hell and the redeemed spirits would float around and sing and twang their harps in a golden city hanging in space in the "Beautiful Isle of Somewhere"! How far away from the plain Bible teaching that is!

I was taught in the Sunday School (and the Theological Semi-nary only strengthened the teaching) that if the meek were ever to inherit the earth, they would have to do it in this life. I was taught that all the promises to Israel really meant the church, and that the promises to Jerusalem and Mount Zion really meant Heaven! I was taught that that golden age—when "they shall beat their swords into plowshares, and their spears into pruning-hooks" (Isa. 2:4; Micah 4:3) and when "the earth shall be full of the knowledge of the Lord, as the waters cover the sea" (Isa. 11:9) —would be brought about by preaching the gospel, aided by schools, hospitals, good laws, peace treaties, inventions and the developments of modern science! I believed that, despite the evi-dences of my senses and the testimony of history and current events, until I began to study the prophetic teachings of the Bible.

Then I learned that God had promised to bring the Israelites back to their land to possess it forever, that Heaven, then, must be on this earth.

If God Set Out to Destroy This World

Let us imagine that to please all our postmillennial and amil-lennial friends, or those of whatever description who have largely ignored the prophetic portions of the Bible, the Lord should pre-pare to burn up and utterly destroy this planet or earth. Let us suppose that, as so many say, the prophecies are highly figurative anyway and that to study and teach or preach them is largely speculation, and so the Lord prepares to strike the match or say the word that will utterly destroy this whole planet. What a multitude is gathered, let us imagine, to behold that great event. But wait! I see an old man who walks like a king who comes forward to interrupt the ceremony. His face has the look of authority and his voice is bold as he cries out, "Wait, Lord; You cannot destroy my property!"

I can imagine the Lord might say, "This man is a friend of mine; let us hear what he has to say. Speak on, friend, tell the people. What is thy name? To what possession do you refer? What title do you hold to the property?"

"My name," says the venerable patriarch, "is Abraham! From Ur of the Chaldees I came at Thy command. To Canaan I came and the land Thou didst give to me, teaching me by faith to know that I should afterward inherit it. To Isaac and Jacob Thou didst make the same promises, and all our days, though rich in gold and silver, cattle and servants, we lived as sojourners and pilgrims in tents, patiently waiting until we should inherit and possess forever our own land. This scroll in my hand, O Lord God, is a written deed to the land of Canaan, called by name, and signed by Thyself. It is a warranty deed; guaranteeing to me and my faithful children after me—the children of promise—the possession of the land forever.

"You may burn up, if You will, the weeds and thorns and thistles. Destroy, if You will, all disease germs and insect pests, which have increased the curse on the land because of man's sin through the centuries. O Lord, You may shake down and burn the cities, for I look for another city which hath foundations whose builder and maker is God. The elements may melt with fervent heat, but the land is mine; to me Thou didst give it with the promise that I should inherit it with my seed. 'Shall not the Judge of all the earth do right?' "

If God wanted to please the ignorant and the scoffers concerning His prophecies, how would He face Abraham? The deed which Abraham has is the Bible, the Word of God.

There will come a time, say the Scriptures, when "the heavens shall pass away with a great noise, and the elements shall melt with fervent heat, the earth also and the works that are therein shall be burned up" (II Pet. 3:10). But the same chapter explains that that will be a judgment like the flood. II Peter 3:6, 7 says:

"Whereby the world that then was, being overflowed with water, perished: But the heavens and the earth, which are now, by the same word are kept in store, reserved unto fire against the day of judgment and perdition of ungodly men."

The world "perished" in the flood. The earth shall be "burned up" in a coming day of judgment. The present heavens or firmament will pass away, we are told, and all that fire can melt on this earth will melt. But as the earth reappeared from the waters of the flood, to be restocked and repopulated and replanted, so in a much greater way this planet, purified of pests, disease, and the marks of sin by the literal fire of God's wrath, will be planted again as the Garden of Eden.

This planet will never be entirely removed, can never cease to be. Psalms 104:5 says: "Who laid the foundations of the earth, that it should not be removed for ever." The fires of judgment will purge this earth, but it will not pass out of existence. It will remain to be the home of God's people through eternity. Canaan shall again be the possession of Abraham and his seed, and at that time they shall possess it forever!

Chapter 3

Israel to Be Restored as a Nation

ONE OF THE greatest themes in the Bible is the promised restoration of Israel to their land, that is, the promise that Israel shall be returned to Palestine and their kingdom re-established. It was this promise that Nehemiah had in mind when he fasted and wept and prayed and took back a remnant to Palestine. It was these great promises that Daniel had in mind when he fasted and wept and prayed and confessed his sin and the sin of his people Israel (Dan. 9:3–19) until God sent him the promise concerning his people Israel and his city Jerusalem, when the transgressions would be finished, sins brought to an end, reconciliation made for iniquity, everlasting righteousness brought in, and the Most Holy One anointed, that is, when the great coming Jewish King should be anointed (Dan. 9:24). This was the hope and promise which the apostles had in mind when they asked the risen Saviour, "Lord, wilt thou at this time restore again the kingdom to Israel?" (Acts 1:6). Peter meant this when he preached that Israel should repent, looking forward to the "times of restitution of all things, which God has spoken by the mouth of all his holy prophets," at the second coming of Christ (Acts 3:19–21). This was the hope of the misguided Zealots when they rebelled against Rome and finally brought about the utter destruction of the city by Titus and the Roman army in A.D. 70.

Israel to Be Dispersed and Later Regathered to Their Land

The twenty-eighth chapter of Deuteronomy is one of the most terrible in the Bible. Almost all of its sixty-eight verses, and most of the twenty-ninth chapter following it, tell of the terrible plagues, the punishment that was to come upon the nation Israel if they should disobey the Lord and forsake His laws. Deuteronomy 28:63–66 makes plain the great dispersion and scattering of Israel among all nations which was to come. As you read it, you will see that it has certainly been fulfilled.

"And it shall come to pass, that as the Lord rejoiced over you to do you good, and to multiply you; so the Lord will rejoice over you to destroy you, and to bring you to nought; and ye shall be plucked from off the land whither thou goest to possess it. 64 And the Lord shall scatter thee among all people, from the one end of the earth even unto the other; and there thou shalt serve other gods, which neither thou nor thy fathers have known, even wood and stone. 65 And among these nations shalt thou find no ease, neither shall the sole of thy foot have rest; but the Lord shall give thee there a trembling heart, and failing of eyes, and sorrow of mind: 66 And thy life shall hang in doubt before thee; and thou shalt fear day and night, and shalt have none assurance of thy life."—Deut. 28:63–66.

Verse 64 shows that this was not merely the Babylonian captivity which God had in mind. They were not to be taken to one nation, but "the Lord shall scatter thee AMONG ALL PEOPLE, FROM THE ONE END OF THE EARTH EVEN UNTO THE OTHER"! No, what God here threatened was that which has come to pass, and is true even today; Jews are scattered in every nation under Heaven. They are in every land and yet have no land of their own, they are among every people, yet they remain a separate people.

Many of Abraham's Seed Destroyed Utterly

That twenty-eighth chapter of Deuteronomy from verse 15 to 68 is full of terrible predictions of the ruin of those Jews who turn away from the Lord God. A careful reading of it makes clear that many Jews have been and will be destroyed without remedy. The promise is not to all of Abraham's seed. In that chapter, verse 20 says that the cursing, vexation and rebuke will be upon them "until thou be destroyed, and until thou perish quickly." Verses 22, 24, 48, 51, and 61 say that the curses of God shall smite wicked, unbelieving Jews "until thou perish" and "until thou be destroyed" etc. It becomes certainly evident that the promises to

Abraham's seed are not for disobedient and rebellious J
plainly told these that they should be destroyed.

But this limitation of the promise was made known fr
very beginning. The Lord told Abraham, "In Isaac shall th ˍˍed
be called" (Gen. 21:12). The promise was not to all of Abraham's
seed, not at all to Ishmael and the sons of Keturah by Abraham.
Later, God chose Jacob and rejected Esau. The "birthright"
which included the covenants and promises was sold by Esau for
a mess of pottage, and profane Esau did not inherit the promises
as did Jacob. The promise to Abraham did not include all of his
descendants.

The Promises Inherited Only by Faith

Romans 4:13 shows that only converted Jews, those who like
Abraham believed in God, shall inherit the Abrahamic promises.
There we are told: "For the promise, that he should be the heir
of the world, was not to Abraham, or to his seed, through the law,
but through the righteousness of faith." The promise was to
Abraham on the basis that he believed God, and the promise to
his seed is on the same basis. Jews who inherit with Abraham
the land of Canaan will inherit it on the basis of righteousness by
faith. Happily, Gentiles also who have the same faith are counted
the seed of Abraham, and will inherit the earth with Abraham
(Gal. 3:7–9, 14, 28, 29). But the point that we are now making is
that only a limited number of all those who have ever descended
from Abraham will inherit the land with Abraham. Those who
inherit will be those who have trusted in the Saviour, as Abraham
did.

That is the reason that half the twenty-eighth chapter of Deuteronomy gives verse after verse saying that Israelites who sinned
should be "destroyed," should "perish." Then verse 63 says:

*"And it shall come to pass, that as the Lord rejoiced over you
to do you good, and to multiply you; so the Lord will rejoice over
you to destroy you, and to bring you to nought; and ye shall be
plucked from off the land whither thou goest to possess it."*

When God threatened to destroy Israelites, He did not mean
that the last Jew would be blotted out, for many Scriptures fore-

tell the eternal existence of the race. But relatively few of the nation have been converted and can inherit the promises.

No Second Chance for Unsaved Jews

Let it be understood that God's plan of salvation for the Jew is the same as for everybody else in the world. Jews are sinners, as are the Gentiles. To be saved, they must turn by faith to Christ as others must do. A Jew who dies unsaved, not having trusted in Christ, does not have any part in the promises made to Abraham. Those promises can be inherited only by those who are heirs through the righteousness of faith (Rom. 4:13). Unrepentant and unbelieving dead, whether Jews or Gentiles, are in Hell and will never be saved. The rich man about whom the Saviour told us in Luke 16:19–31 was a Jew, an unsaved Jew, who in Hell yet called Abraham his father, as he literally was, that is, his ancestor.

Unbelieving Jews Not Really Abraham's Seed

How could unbelieving Jews inherit promises of God made to the spiritually-minded, believing Abraham, the child of God, the friend and prophet of God? Jesus plainly told the unsaved Pharisees of His day that though they were physically descended from Abraham, they were not really Abraham's seed but were children of the Devil (John 8:37–44). John the Baptist preached that "God is able of these stones to raise up children unto Abraham" (Matt. 3:9).

Even when the whole remnant of Israel is converted, each individual must put his faith in Jesus as the Saviour, the only way anyone has ever been saved, or ever will be saved. A nation shall be born at once (Isa. 66:8), "and so all Israel shall be saved" (Rom. 11:26); but that will come when individual Jews all turn, as they one day will, to receive the Saviour and trust Him as their Messiah, their Deliverer, and their King.

The Regathering of Israel and the Future Foretold

After all the warnings of the terrible punishment God would bring on Israel when they forgot God, it is refreshing to know that He will one day turn their hearts back again. Israel has been dispersed. Israel will be regathered. God has not cast away His people.

Deuteronomy 30:1–6 is a very important passage showing God's plan for Israel in the future. When you read it carefully, I will call attention to several important facts in that passage.

"And it shall come to pass, when all these things are come upon thee, the blessing and the curse, which I have set before thee, and thou shalt call them to mind among all the nations, whither the Lord thy God hath driven thee, 2 And shalt return unto the Lord thy God, and shalt obey his voice according to all that I command thee this day, thou and thy children, with all thine heart, and with all thy soul; 3 That then the Lord thy God will turn thy captivity, and have compassion upon thee, and will return and gather thee from all the nations, whither the Lord thy God hath scattered thee. 4 If any of thine be driven out unto the outmost parts of heaven, from thence will the Lord thy God gather thee, and from thence will he fetch thee: 5 And the Lord thy God will bring thee into the land which thy fathers possessed, and thou shalt possess it; and he will do thee good, and multiply thee above thy fathers. 6 And the Lord thy God will circumcise thine heart, and the heart of thy seed, to love the Lord thy God with all thine heart, and with all thy soul, that thou mayest live."
—Deut. 30:1–6.

Notice the following great facts which are made clear in this passage: (1) God does not say "if," but "when." God knew that the sins of Israel would lead to their being scattered in all the world. (2) He also knew that far later those of the nation yet alive would be led to return to the Lord as told in verse 2. In the inspired words of Moses, Israel will return to obey the very commandments in these Mosaic laws. (This will be in the Great Tribulation period to come, as you will later see.) (3) The nation Israel will be regathered to their own land. Verse 4 makes clear that every living Jew "driven out unto the outmost parts of heaven" will be gathered and brought back to the land of Canaan. Notice particularly that verse 5 says, "And the Lord thy God will bring thee into the land which thy fathers possessed, and thou shalt possess it." The fathers of present day Jews possessed the land of Israel, but they did not have EVERLASTING possession of it. In the future, every living Jew under Heaven will be brought back to the land of Canaan to possess it. (4) This

Scripture above makes clear that after the Israelites are gathered back to their own land, then they will not merely keep the law of Moses, but they will be "circumcised in heart." They will be converted, born again, and have everlasting life.

Ezekiel Reveals the Hope of Israel

Many times in Ezekiel do we find this theme of the restoration of Israel to their own land, Palestine. Chapters 34, 36 and 37 are especially plain. God is the Shepherd and the children of Israel are His people. Ezekiel 34:11–13 says:

"For thus saith the Lord God; Behold, I, even I, will both search my sheep, and seek them out. As a shepherd seeketh out his flock in the day that he is among his sheep that are scattered; so will I seek out my sheep, and will deliver them out of all places where they have been scattered in the cloudy and dark day. And I will bring them out from the people, and gather them from the countries, and will bring them to their own land, and feed them upon the mountains of Israel by the rivers, and in all the inhabited places of the country."

The prophecy is about Israel; they will be brought "to their own land," Palestine, the land of "the mountains of Israel." This is not figurative, but literal.

Again in Ezekiel 36:22–28 we find a plain promise from God to Israel that they will be regathered from among the heathen, gathered out of all countries, and brought again "INTO YOUR OWN LAND," that then they will be given new hearts, or converted.

"Therefore say unto the house of Israel, Thus saith the Lord God; I do not this for your sakes, O house of Israel, but for mine holy name's sake, which ye have profaned among the heathen, whither ye went. And I will sanctify my great name, which was profaned among the heathen, which ye have profaned in the midst of them; and the heathen shall know that I am the Lord, saith the Lord God, when I shall be sanctified in you before their eyes. For I will take you from among the heathen, and gather you out of all countries, and will bring you into YOUR OWN LAND. Then will I sprinkle clean water upon you, and ye shall

be clean: from all your filthiness, and from all your idols, will I cleanse you. A new heart also will I give you, and a new spirit will I put within you: and I will take away the stony heart out of your flesh, and I will give you an heart of flesh. And I will put my spirit within you, and cause you to walk in my statutes, and ye shall keep my judgments, and do them. AND YE SHALL DWELL IN THE LAND THAT I GAVE TO YOUR FA- THERS; and ye shall be my people, and I will be your God."

—Ezek. 36:22-28.

This passage, like Deuteronomy 30:1-6, plainly promises that all of Israel left alive on the earth will one day be restored to Palestine, their own land, that there they will be converted and there will enter into the everlasting possession which God prom- ised them. Do not call this figurative language, nor explain away the meaning. The Lord plainly says, "And ye shall dwell in the land that I gave to your fathers," the literal land Canaan. If there should be any doubt, the remainder of the chapter tells of the increase of corn, the tilling of the land, the building of cities and that the whole land shall be like the Garden of Eden (Ezek. 36:35). The Lord is not here talking about some mystic, unreal place out in space where disembodied spirits gather. He is talking about a literal land, with soil that grows crops, a land where cities are built and prosper. The place is the land of Palestine where people will be regathered with literal bodies to eat, drink, sow and reap, build and inhabit, a physical Garden of Eden, a literal Heaven upon earth.

The Valley of Dry Bones

In the thirty-seventh chapter, Ezekiel saw a vision, a valley of dry bones, very, very dry. In the vision Ezekiel was commanded to prophesy to these dry bones that they should live, and as he prophesied, there was a noise and shaking and the bones came together, sinews and flesh came upon them and skin, and then the wind brought breath into these bodies, and they lived, an exceeding great army! Then the Lord explained the vision in the following words:

"Then he said unto me, Son of man, these bones are the whole house of Israel: behold, they say, Our bones are dried, and our

hope is lost: we are cut off for our parts. Therefore prophesy and say unto them, Thus saith the Lord God; Behold, O my people, I will open your graves, and cause you to come up out of your graves, and bring you into the land of Israel. And ye shall know that I am the Lord, when I have opened your graves, O my people, and brought you up out of your graves, And shall put my spirit in you, and ye shall live, and I shall place you in your own land: then shall ye know that I the Lord have spoken it, and performed it, saith the Lord."—Ezek. 37:11–14.

The bones are not the bones of the dead, but the bones of the living. The graves are the countries all over the world where Jews are scattered and buried alive. Israel as a nation seems dead, but God will revive national Israel again. God is not talking ABOUT Israel, but TO Israel. It is important to notice that though God here uses a figure of speech, He plainly states what the figure pictures. He says, "These bones are the whole house of Israel." The resurrection here pictured, then, is the resurrection of "the whole house of Israel." God hears the despairing cry of the Jews as they say, "Our bones are dried, and our hope is lost: we are cut off for our parts." Many Israelites mourn as did Daniel and Nehemiah over their state; no king, no priesthood, no sacrifice; cast out of their land, persecuted around the world. To these God says, "Behold, O my people, I will open your graves, and cause you to come up out of your graves, and bring you into the land of Israel." God is speaking here to living Jews but about their national deadness. It is a promise to the literal people, Israel, of their restoration as a nation to their land and to the favor of God.

The breath that will come into Israel will be the return of the Spirit of God to spiritually dead Israel. The resurrection He promises here is the return to their own land from the graves which are other countries. Notice again the plain, literal promise in verse 14, "And I shall place you in YOUR OWN LAND." Israel, that is, living Jews, will be restored to their own land as a literal nation again.

The Sign of the Two Sticks

In the rest of the same thirty-seventh chapter of Ezekiel, God showed through the prophet the reuniting of the two kingdoms,

Judah and the ten tribes, the Northern and Southern kingdoms, which divided in the days of Rehoboam, Solomon's son. Notice how literal are these promises. Notice the promise about Christ, the greater David, the Descendant of David. See that the happy land promised is not a heaven on some other planet, but literal Palestine. Here is the rest of the chapter, Ezekiel 37:15–28:

"The word of the Lord came again unto me, saying, 16 More-over, thou son of man, take thee one stick, and write upon it, For Judah, and for the children of Israel his companions: then take another stick, and write upon it, For Joseph, the stick of Ephraim, and for all the house of Israel his companions: 17 And join them one to another into one stick; and they shall become one in thine hand. 18 And when the children of thy people shall speak unto thee, saying, Wilt thou not shew us what thou meanest by these? 19 Say unto them, Thus saith the Lord God; Behold, I will take the stick of Joseph, which is in the hand of Ephraim, and the tribes of Israel his fellows, and will put them with him, even with the stick of Judah, and make them one stick, and they shall be one in mine hand. 20 And the sticks whereon thou writest shall be in thine hand before their eyes. 21 And say unto them, Thus saith the Lord God; Behold, I will take the children of Israel from among the heathen, whither they be gone, and will gather them on every side, and BRING THEM INTO THEIR OWN LAND: 22 AND I WILL MAKE THEM ONE NATION IN THE LAND UPON THE MOUNTAINS OF ISRAEL; and one king shall be king to them all: and they shall be no more two nations, neither shall they be divided into two kingdoms any more at all: 23 Neither shall they defile themselves any more with their idols, nor with their detestable things, nor with any of their transgressions: but I will save them out of all their dwelling places, wherein they have sinned, and will cleanse them: so shall they be my people, and I will be their God. 24 And David my servant shall be king over them; and they all shall have one shepherd: they shall also walk in my judgments, and observe my statutes, and do them. 25 And they shall dwell IN THE LAND THAT I HAVE GIVEN UNTO JACOB MY SERVANT, WHEREIN YOUR FATHERS HAVE DWELT; AND THEY SHALL DWELL THEREIN, EVEN THEY, AND THEIR

CHILDREN, AND THEIR CHILDREN'S CHILDREN FOR EVER: and my servant David shall be their prince for ever. 26 Moreover I will make a covenant of peace with them; it shall be an everlasting covenant with them: and I will place them, and multiply them, and will set my sanctuary in the midst of them for evermore. 27 My tabernacle also shall be with them: yea, I will be their God, and they shall be my people. 28 And the heathen shall know that I the Lord do sanctify Israel, when my sanctuary shall be in the midst of them for evermore."

Do you not see why Jews in the time of Christ expected Him to set up a literal kingdom? Do you not see why they expected it to be in the land of Canaan, "on the mountains of Israel?" Many, many times are these plain promises given by the prophets in the Old Testament.

"For Ever," "For Ever," "Everlasting Covenant," "For Evermore," "For Evermore"

In the above Scripture, Ezekiel 37, especially verses 25 to 28, the Lord emphatically repeats His statement that the restoration of Israel to the land of Canaan shall be for an everlasting possession. Five times in these four verses does the Lord mention the eternal character of this restoration of Israel.

They shall dwell in the land of Canaan "for ever" (v. 25).

And the greater David shall be their prince "for ever" (v. 25).

The covenant God will make them will be "an everlasting covenant" (v. 26).

God will set His sanctuary in the midst of them "for evermore" (v. 26).

Again we are told the temple or sanctuary will be in the midst of them "for evermore" (v. 28).

The promise to Abraham was forever and so is the promise to the nation Israel. When Israel is restored to their land to possess it, they will possess it for evermore.

The land, the kingdom, the covenant, the sanctuary of God, all of these shall be enjoyed forever "in the land that I have given unto Jacob my servant, wherein your fathers have dwelt."

The Return From Babylon Did Not Fulfill This Prophecy

The promises which we have read in Ezekiel were not fulfilled when the children of Israel returned from their captivity in

Babylon. Those Jews did not stay in their land forever. God's sanctuary did not abide there forever, but the temple was destroyed in A.D. 70, and since that time Jews have been scattered to all parts of the earth.

Nor were the Jews converted (that is, the entire nation) at that time. In the passage used above to show the promised restoration of Israel to their land, we were clearly told that Israel should be wonderfully converted.

Ezekiel 36:26, 27, mentioned above, tells of this conversion.

"A new heart also will I give you, and a new spirit will I put within you: and I will take away the stony heart out of your flesh, and I will give you an heart of flesh. And I will put my spirit within you, and cause you to walk in my statutes, and ye shall keep my judgments, and do them."

Just before and just after these two verses in the same passage, we read how God was to restore Israel to their land. When the children of Israel were brought back from the Babylonian captivity then we could not say that every individual Jew had a change of heart. Nothing like that is said in Nehemiah and Ezra which describes their return from captivity. Many of those Jews doubtless were saved, but never yet has there been a nation on the earth, as far as we know, in which every individual was a child of God.

Above we studied Ezekiel 37:15–28 where the Lord instructed Ezekiel to take two sticks and bind them together until they should be one and say to the people that one day He would bring back Judah and Israel and make them one nation in the land on the mountains of Israel forever. In the midst of that passage, now notice verse 23.

"Neither shall they defile themselves any more with their idols, nor with their detestable things, nor with any of their transgressions: but I will save them out of all their dwellingplaces, wherein they have sinned, and will cleanse them: so shall they be my people, and I will be their God."

That verse says that when Israel is restored to their land forever, they never again shall defile themselves with idols nor detestable things "nor WITH ANY OF THEIR TRANSGRESSIONS." In other words, the Scripture makes clear that Israel will never again turn away from God nor sin against Him when they are brought back to the land of Canaan and restored again as a nation to God's favor, for they will be saved and not only saved but glorified.

Certainly then, that restoration mentioned in these Scriptures and prophesied for Israel was not the restoration from their Babylonian captivity. Israel since that time has clearly sinned. They have rejected and crucified their own Messiah or Saviour, the Lord Jesus Christ. For their sins they have now been scattered from one end of Heaven to the other, around the world.

Israel to Be Regathered Out of "All Countries," Not Just Out of Babylon

The restoration of Israel to their land which we are discussing is a far more general and universal restoration than that which happened when Israel went back from Babylon to their land. In that day the total number who went back, as given in Ezra 2:64–65 and Nehemiah 7:66–67, was only about 50,000. Probably many more Israelites were in the land of Babylon who preferred not to return to Canaan. Most of those who went back were of the tribe of Judah though some were from every tribe. Those who returned were a remnant of the nation.

How much greater will be the return to Palestine when God restores the whole nation again as pictured in His Word.

In Deuteronomy 30:3–5 speaking on this matter, remember that the Lord said:

"Then the Lord thy God will turn thy captivity, and have compassion upon thee, and will return and gather thee from all the nations, whither the Lord thy God hath scattered thee. If any of thine be driven out unto the outmost parts of heaven, from thence will the Lord thy God gather thee, and from thence will he fetch thee: And the Lord thy God will bring thee into the land which thy fathers possessed, and thou shalt possess it; and he will do thee good, and multiply thee above thy fathers."

This Scripture plainly indicates that God will gather every living Jew under Heaven back to the land of Palestine! Verse 3 says that the Lord "will return and gather thee from ALL THE NATIONS," not simply from the region of Babylon. Even from "the outmost parts of heaven" the Lord will gather Israelites to bring them back to their land. Ezekiel 36:24 says: "For I will take you from among the heathen, and gather you OUT OF ALL COUNTRIES, and will bring you into your own land." Ezekiel 37:21 says that "I will take the children of Israel from among the heathen, whither they be gone, and will gather them ON EVERY SIDE, and bring them into their own land." The regathering of Israel prophesied will include every Jew alive in every nation on earth. Nothing like this happened in the days of the return from Babylon with Ezra and Nehemiah.

From Babylon Jews "Returned"; at The Restoration God Will "Gather" Them

When some Israelites under Nehemiah and Ezra returned to Palestine to rebuild the walls of Jerusalem and their temple, King Cyrus made a proclamation stating that all Israelites who wished might return to their land (II Chronicles 36:22, 23; Ezra 1:1-4). They went of their own accord. Those who chose to return, returned. Those who chose to remain where they were, remained.

So it has been since that time. The Zionist movement is a movement sponsored by unconverted Jews with a laudable purpose of restoring some Jews to their own land, Palestine. Those who are successful, prosperous and happy in other nations around the world remain where they are. Those who are unhappy, and long to go back to Palestine are encouraged to go. The movement rests on the will of men, not the will of God. The new national Israel is only a fragment and is not a fulfillment of the prophecies about Israel being restored. Preachers who think so are mistaken.

The capture of Jerusalem in 1917 by General Allenby whereby Palestine was opened to control by the British and colonization by Jews, was of no significance in the promised restoration of Israel to their land. The stream of immigration whereby Jewish people dribble back to Palestine in this day does not fulfill the wonderful promises of God. First, as we have shown, this does not include all the Jews in all countries, even to the outmost parts of Heaven, and second, in this movement men are the active ones, and not God.

As long as it is left to the will of men, we can expect that Jews will be found in every nation in the world. Their enterprise, their foresight, their thrift will carry them wherever there is business for bankers, traders, merchants, peddlers, capitalists, scientists, artists, musicians, and statesmen, but when God's time comes He will turn the hearts of the people back toward the land and then He Himself "will gather them on every side and bring them into their own land."

Chapter 4

When Will Israel Be Regathered and Converted? At Christ's Coming!

$\mathcal{S}$URELY IT IS an established teaching of the Word of God that Israel will all be restored to their land. As to that, the promises are clear. When, then, will Israel be carried back to their land as a nation under the blessing of God to inherit their eternal possession? The Scriptures give the answer that it will be at the second coming of Christ. No past movement of the people of Israel to Palestine fulfills the prophecies, and in the Bible, the restoration is repeatedly connected with the conversion of the entire remnant of the nation and the beginning of the reign of Christ as His Second Coming.

Here is one of the simplest proofs that Christ's kingdom has not been set up on the earth. In dozens of places in the Bible we are taught that the coming kingdom will follow the regathering of Israel to their own land, Canaan. In II Samuel 7:10, the Lord revealed to David through the prophet Nathan His plan for the regathering of Israel and their settling in "a place of their own" to move no more, in the following words: "Moreover I will appoint a place for my people Israel, and will plant them, that they may dwell in a place of their own, and move no more; neither shall the children of wickedness afflict them any more, as beforetime." Then in the following verses, II Samuel 7:11–16, the Lord gave David the great covenant about his dynasty and the everlasting kingdom. The kingdom follows the regathering of Israel to their own land. God will place Israel permanently in their own land and then David's Descendant will reign over them on David's throne.

The Scripture in Isaiah 11:10–12 plainly says that the coming of the great King, "a root of Jesse," that is, the Descendant of David and his father Jesse, will be *IN THE SAME DAY* as the regathering of Israel.

> *"And IN THAT DAY there shall be a root of Jesse, which shall stand for an ensign of the people; to it shall the Gentiles seek: and his rest shall be glorious. 11 And it shall come to pass IN THAT DAY, that the Lord shall set his hand again the second time to recover the remnant of his people, which shall be left, from Assyria, and from Egypt, and from Pathros, and from Cush, and from Elam, and from Shinar, and from Hamath, and from the islands of the sea. 12 And he shall set up an ensign for the nations, and shall assemble the outcasts of Israel, and gather together the dispersed of Judah from the four corners of the earth."*
> —Isa. 11:10–12.

Note in verse 11 the exact words "in that day." The beginning of the reign of Christ and the assembling of the outcasts of Israel from every corner of the earth will take place in the same day.

Jeremiah 23:3–6 again connects the raising up of the "righteous BRANCH" of David to reign on David's throne with the regathering of the children of Israel. When God gathers His flock, Israel, out of all countries and brings them again to their own fold, then the Lord Jesus "shall reign and prosper, and shall execute judgment and justice in the earth." The same thing is promised in Jeremiah 33:14–17.

In Ezekiel, chapter 34, read verses 12 to 14 and 22 to 24. The order is the same. God will regather Israel, and then the kingdom of David will be restored. Ezekiel 37:21–25 shows the same thing again.

The Regathering of Israel for the Kingdom to Take Place at Christ's Second Coming

We have taken detailed steps to impress it upon your heart, but ere this you must have seen that the regathering of Israel is one great, sudden event at the second coming of Christ. That is exactly what the Scripture teaches. In Matthew 24:29–31, the Saviour gives the order of events. Following a Great Tribulation on this earth, He will return visibly and personally to this earth.

Then He shall send His angels and regather His elect or chosen people of Israel.

> *"Immediately after the tribulation of those days shall the sun be darkened, and the moon shall not give her light, and the stars shall fall from heaven, and the powers of the heavens shall be shaken: And then shall appear the sign of the Son of man in heaven: and then shall all the tribes of the earth mourn, and they shall see the Son of man coming in the clouds of heaven with power and great glory. And he shall send his angels with a great sound of a trumpet, and they shall gather together his elect from the four winds, from one end of heaven to the other."*
> —Matt. 24:29–31.

This Scripture fits with all the others concerning the regathering of Israel and the establishment of His kingdom. Christ the King will gather His flock, and establish His kingdom over them, on the mountains of Israel. This, Jesus Himself said, did not happen at His first coming, but would happen on His visible, bodily return to this earth. The slow migration of Jewish people back to Palestine cannot fulfill this Scripture, but with all the authority of the Son of God upon them, the angels of Heaven will scatter to all the world to seek out every living Jew and bring him back to the land of his fathers, to meet his promised King, the Lord Jesus Christ! The regathering of Israel to Palestine waits for the second coming of Christ.

Then will come the blessed kingdom of Christ, when "He shall reign over the house of Jacob for ever" (Luke 1:33).

Israel Will Be Saved When Regathered

The kingdom of Christ awaits not only the regathering of Israel, but their conversion as well. Since the Jewish nation rejected Christ at His first coming, most of the Jews were not saved then, and since most Jews have not been Christians in any age since Jesus came, it is certain that Christ's kingdom has not been set up on the earth. Those who do not take the promises about Christ's kingdom on earth literally, but explain them away, teach that Christ set up His kingdom at His first coming, or, as some teach, at Pentecost. But they overlook many Scriptures which positively teach that at the establishment of Christ's kingdom on earth the Jewish nation will be converted.

Jews to Be "Circumcised in Heart"

Connected with the promise of the regathering of Israel for their kingdom, at a number of places in the Bible is a statement that they will be circumcised in heart, or converted. Deuteronomy 30:5, 6 speaks of this as follows:

"And the Lord thy God will bring thee into the land which thy fathers possessed, and thou shalt possess it; and he will do thee good, and multiply thee above thy fathers. And the Lord thy God WILL CIRCUMCISE THINE HEART, AND THE HEART OF THY SEED, TO LOVE THE LORD THY GOD WITH ALL THINE HEART, AND WITH ALL THY SOUL, that thou mayest live."

Circumcision among Jews always meant that they were a chosen, separate people, set apart according to the plan of God. Actually, circumcision ought to have been, and with spiritual Jews was, a sign that they were wholly set apart to love and serve the true God. A Jew who has been circumcised in the flesh is set apart physically as one of God's chosen race, Israel. But as long as he rejects the Jewish Messiah, he belies his circumcision. He is not circumcised in heart. When with all his heart he turns to seek the Lord, and finds Him, then the Jew, born again, a child of God, is truly 'circumcised in heart!' In this passage we are told that the circumcision of heart for all the Jews will be in connection with their regathering to their own land. Circumcision of Israelites in the Old Testament plainly signified separation, and said, 'This man is different, he is God's man!' That circumcision only faintly foretold the time when Israelites would be circumcised in heart, when every living Jew would know and love the true God.

Ezekiel 36:24–27 tells us again of this coming time when Jews shall have a change of heart when they are regathered to Palestine. Remember that this regathering is connected everywhere with the kingdom of David, and the kingdom of Israel cannot be restored until Israel is saved.

"For I will take you from among the heathen, and gather you out of all countries, and will bring you into your own land. Then

*will I sprinkle clean water upon you, and ye shall be clean: from
all your filthiness, and from all your idols, will I cleanse you. A
new heart also will I give you, and a new spirit will I put within
you: and I will take away the stony heart out of your flesh, and I
will give you an heart of flesh. And I will put my spirit within
you, and cause you to walk in my statutes, and ye shall keep my
judgments, and do them."*—Ezek. 36:24–27.

This Scripture is as clear a picture of salvation as "ye must be
born again."

"A new heart," "a new Spirit" will be given Jews when they
are regathered for the kingdom of Christ and are in their own
land. This is the same individual salvation that Christians have
today.

Read again Ezekiel 37:15–28 where the Lord instructed Ezekiel
to take two sticks and bind them together until they should be
one and to say to the people that one day He would bring back
Judah and Israel and make them one nation in the land on
the mountains of Israel forever. In the midst of that passage, now
see verse 23:

*"Neither shall they defile themselves any more with their idols,
nor with their detestable things, nor with any of their transgressions: but I will save them out of all their dwellingplaces, wherein
they have sinned, and will cleanse them: so shall they be my people, and I will be their God."*

Israel to Be Saved Then

Do not miss the blessed significance of this passage. Verse 23
tells us about Israelites that, "I WILL SAVE THEM OUT OF
ALL THEIR DWELLINGPLACES, WHEREIN THEY HAVE
SINNED, AND WILL CLEANSE THEM: SO SHALL THEY
BE MY PEOPLE, AND I WILL BE THEIR GOD." That
plainly refers to salvation. Verses 26, 27 and 28 say that God will
set His sanctuary, His tabernacle, in the midst of them forever-
more. He will be their God, and Israel shall be His people! That
verse says that when Israel is restored to their land forever they
shall never again defile themselves with idols nor detestable
things, "NOR WITH ANY OF THEIR TRANSGRESSIONS."
In other words, the Scripture makes clear that Israel will never

again turn away from God nor sin against Him when they are brought back to the land of Canaan and restored again as a nation to God's favor, for they will be saved, and not only saved but glorified.

Paul in his inspired letter to the church at Rome tells us more about this coming conversion of Israel. In Romans 11:25–27 we are told that the conversion of the whole nation Israel will be after the fulness of the Gentiles comes in and that "all Israel shall be saved" when Jesus the Deliverer comes again to reign.

> *"For I would not, brethren, that ye should be ignorant of this mystery, lest ye should be wise in your own conceits; that blindness in part is happened to Israel, until the fulness of the Gentiles be come in. And so all Israel shall be saved: as it is written, There shall come out of Sion the Deliverer, and shall turn away ungodliness from Jacob: For this is my covenant unto them, when I shall take away their sins."*—Rom. 11:25–27.

In the preceding verses of the same chapter, Paul tells us how present-day Israel, branches of the tame olive tree to whom God gave His great and precious promises, have been broken off because of unbelief, while we, the Gentiles, the wild olive branches, have been grafted in. But when the fulness of the Gentiles be come in, that is, when most of the Gentiles who will be saved are saved, then the Lord Jesus will return and appear unto Israel, and they will recognize and love and trust Him and be saved. "All Israel shall be saved." That had not happened yet when Paul wrote. It has never happened since. It awaits the second coming of Christ.

This church or gospel age is the time of the "fulness of the Gentiles." The fulness of the Gentiles must come before the time comes for all Israel to be saved. Now most Christians are Gentiles, and relatively few Jews today have accepted Jesus as their Messiah and Saviour. But when the fulness of the Gentiles is come in, and when Israel is restored to their land as pictured in the Scriptures above, then "ALL ISRAEL SHALL BE SAVED!" When He, the Deliverer, comes to deliver Israel from the armies of the Antichrist and restore them to their own land, then Israel shall be saved.

Here, to me, is one of the most fascinating themes of all the

Bible, that Jesus should be loved by His own people, should be sought by the race that rejected Him, that they should mourn for Him and seek Him, and then, praise God, find Him! That is one of the most interesting stories in the Bible, and it is clearly told so all can read it who will.

The book of Zechariah is packed full of prophecies concerning the return of the Saviour and the conversion of Israel. Chapter 14 tells of the return of Christ in power with all His saints, to deliver the Jews, when the Antichrist and his armies shall have besieged Jerusalem and have taken it. That chapter tells how "his feet shall stand in that day upon the mount of Olives," how in one day the Lord shall defeat the armies of the nations of this world, and then how "the Lord shall be king over all the earth." That chapter clearly tells of the setting up of the kingdom of Christ on earth. But in the preceding chapters we find scattered the divine prophecies of the conviction and conversion of Israel.

Israel to Mourn Over Their Sins

Zechariah 12:10–14 shows that a deep conviction for sin shall come upon Israelites when they first see the returned Saviour "whom they have pierced." By that time Israel will have had enough of her rebellion, and when they see the Saviour they will mourn over Him, we are told, "as one mourneth for his only son."

"And I will pour upon the house of David, and upon the inhabitants of Jerusalem, the spirit of grace and of supplications: and they shall look upon me whom they have pierced, and they shall mourn for him, as one mourneth for his only son, and shall be in bitterness for him, as one that is in bitterness for his firstborn. In that day shall there be a great mourning in Jerusalem, as the mourning of Hadadrimmon in the valley of Megiddon. And the land shall mourn, every family apart; the family of the house of David apart, and their wives apart; the family of the house of Nathan apart, and their wives apart; The family of the house of Levi apart, and their wives apart; the family of Shimei apart, and their wives apart; All the families that remain, every family apart, and their wives apart."—Zech. 12:10–14.

Zechariah 13:1, 2, 6 follow immediately, so we print it here before we comment.

"In that day there shall be a fountain opened to the house of David and to the inhabitants of Jerusalem for sin and for uncleanness. And it shall come to pass in that day, saith the Lord of hosts, that I will cut off the names of the idols out of the land, and they shall no more be remembered: and also I will cause the prophets and the unclean spirit to pass out of the land."

"And one shall say unto him, What are these wounds in thine hands? Then he shall answer, Those with which I was wounded in the house of my friends."

Jesus will open the fountain for sin and uncleanness to all Israel when He returns to reign! When the people Israel, the nation that condemned Him to be pierced with thorns and nails and spear, see Him, they will mourn over Him in sincerest sorrow for sin. They will ask, "What are these wounds in thine hands?" and He will answer, "Those with which I was wounded in the house of my friends." They will need no further proof that He is the Messiah than His marvelous coming to fulfill the prophecies, regather Israel and establish His kingdom. So then it will come to pass that "All Israel shall be saved."

This conversion of what is left alive of the nation Israel must take place at the second coming of Christ. It has not happened yet, and that is all the more certain proof that Christ has not yet established His kingdom, but that it will be established at the Second Coming.

Chapter 5

David's Kingdom Over Israel to Be Restored Forever

THERE ARE three great elements in all prophecies of the future. They are: a land, a people, and a throne or kingdom. The land is Palestine or Canaan, the people, Israel, and the throne is the throne of David. In II Samuel 7:8–16 we are plainly told that all these elements will be combined when the nation Israel is brought back to their own land and established there forever under the kingdom of a Descendant of David on David's throne. Nathan the prophet was sent by the Lord to tell David that the throne of his kingdom would be established forever over Israel in the future. Read this passage with this in mind.

"Now therefore so shalt thou say unto my servant David, Thus saith the Lord of hosts, I took thee from the sheepcote, from following the sheep, to be ruler over my people, over Israel: 9 And I was with thee whithersoever thou wentest, and have cut off all thine enemies out of thy sight, and have made thee a great name, like unto the name of the great men that are in the earth. 10 Moreover I will appoint a place for my people Israel, and will plant them, that they may dwell in a place of their own, and move no more; neither shall the children of wickedness afflict them any more, as beforetime, 11 And as since the time that I commanded judges to be over my people Israel, and have caused thee to rest from all thine enemies. Also the Lord telleth thee that he will make thee an house. 12 And when thy days be fulfilled, and thou shalt sleep with thy fathers, I will set up thy seed after thee, which shall proceed out of thy bowels, and I will establish his kingdom. 13 He shall build an house for my name, and I will establish the

*throne of his kingdom for ever. 14 I will be his father, and he
shall be my son. If he commit iniquity, I will chasten him with
the rod of men, and with the stripes of the children of men:
15 But my mercy shall not depart away from him, as I took it
from Saul, whom I put away before thee. 16 And thine house and
thy kingdom shall be established for ever before thee: thy throne
shall be established for ever."*—II Sam. 7:8–16.

Verse 10 says a surprising thing! Israel was already in the land
of promise, Palestine or Canaan, and David's throne was already
established there, and he was their king, yet the promise is "Moreover I WILL appoint a place for my people Israel, and WILL
plant them, that they may dwell in a place of their own, and move
no more." Years after the death of David, Israel would be carried
to Babylon, and later scattered all over the world. David's kingdom, then established, would be temporarily discontinued in the
captivity and afterward. In the time of Christ there was no king
on the throne of David; even today there is none. There has been
no descendant of David reigning on a throne at Jerusalem over a
nation Israel now for these more than 2,000 years! So the Lord
promised David that in the future, when Israel would be regathered, He would "appoint a place for my people Israel, and will
plant them, that they may dwell in a place of their own, and move
no more; neither shall the children of wickedness afflict them any
more, as beforetime."

Verses 11 to 15 make clear that God promised David He would
establish David's kingly line so that whatever should happen,
David's dynasty would not be broken up forever as was the dynasty of King Saul. When Solomon and other kings descended
from David did sin against God, verses 14 and 15 promise that the
one sinning would be chastened and whipped, but that it would
not break God's covenant.

Then verse 16 repeats, "And thine house and thy kingdom shall
be established for ever before thee: thy throne shall be established
for ever." The dynasty of David, in the future, was to be established forever. There would come a time when a King of David's
line would rule on David's throne forever.

When will David's kingdom be re-established? When will this
coming Son of David take up the throne? In this passage, the

Lord plainly connects two great events: the return of Israel to their own land, and the re-establishment of the throne of David. In verse 10, God said to David, "Moreover I will appoint a place for my people Israel, and will plant them, that they may dwell in a place of their own, and move no more," and then shows the promise of the unending reign of David's dynasty. The two are inevitably connected. This is the same time as discussed in Deuteronomy 30:5, where the Lord promises, "And the Lord thy God will bring thee into the land which thy fathers possessed, and thou shalt possess it." The regathering of Israel, the re-establishment of David's throne, and the conversion of Israel are three inseparably connected events. First Chronicles, chapter 17, gives a very full and interesting account of this marvelous covenant of God with David, promising the eternal establishment of David's throne and with a Descendant of David upon it. Much of it is given in the same words of this passage in II Samuel 7:10-16, but you should carefully read it. Line upon line God made sure His promises.

Eighty-Ninth Psalm Repeats Covenant With David

This covenant with David is referred to many times in the Bible. In the eighty-ninth Psalm are several plain statements about this covenant. Verses 3 and 4 say: "I have made a covenant with my chosen. I have sworn unto David my servant, Thy seed will I establish for ever, and build up thy throne to all generations. Selah" (Psalm 89:3, 4). The seed of David and the throne of David are to be established and built up forever, even "to all generations." In the same eighty-ninth Psalm, verse 27 to 37 say:

"Also I will make him my firstborn, higher than the kings of the earth. 28 My mercy will I keep for him for evermore, and my covenant shall stand fast with him. 29 His seed also will I make to endure for ever, and his throne as the days of heaven. 30 If his children forsake my law, and walk not in my judgments; 31 If they break my statutes, and keep not my commandments; 32 Then will I visit their transgression with the rod, and their iniquity with stripes. 33 Nevertheless my lovingkindness will I not utterly take from him, nor suffer my faithfulness to fail. 34 My covenant will I not break, nor alter the thing that is gone out of my lips. 35 Once have I sworn by my holiness that I will not lie unto

*David. 36 His seed shall endure for ever, and his throne as the
sun before me. 37 It shall be established for ever as the moon, and
as a faithful witness in heaven. Selah."*—Psalm 89:27–37.

Verse 27 clearly teaches that the coming King, of the seed of
David, is to be higher than all the kings of the earth. He is to be
Ruler with worldwide sway and with an everlasting kingdom.
Verses 30 to 35 plainly say that however the kings of Israel and
Judah following David were to sin, that God would not break
His covenant or promise with David, would not cast off the Da-
vidic dynasty under any circumstances. There are no conditions
to this promise. It is attested by the sworn oath of God Himself
(v. 36), that the Seed of David "shall endure for ever and his
throne as the sun before me."

If we honestly accept these plain promises of God, we must believe that the throne upon which David sat at Jerusalem will be
re-established and will endure forever, and that on this throne at
Jerusalem will sit this great Son of David, literally descended
from his loins.

David's Kingdom, a Tree Cut Down, to Grow Again

More than once in the Bible an earthly and literal kingdom is
pictured and symbolized by a tree. In Ezekiel 31:3 the Assyrian
king is pictured as a great cedar tree, and the symbol is carried
out throughout the chapter. In verse 18 the same symbol is used
to picture Pharaoh of Egypt. The cutting down of the tree there
means the destruction of the kingdom. In Daniel 4:10–27, we are
told how God gave to Nebuchadnezzar the dream of a great tree
which pictured his own rule as a world emperor. The tree, in the
dream, was cut down, but the stump was left. The inspired interpretation is that Nebuchadnezzar would lose his kingdom for a
time to dwell among the beasts of the field, but that when his
heart was humble, God would restore his kingdom.

The same image is used more than once in the Bible concerning the kingdom of David. David's kingdom was established and
grew into a great tree. When Israel and Judah were carried into
captivity, the kingdom was destroyed until only the stump remains. David's kingly seed remains, but his throne at Jerusalem
is vacant. But out of the stump of David's once proud kingdom
grows a Sprout, a Branch who will restore in multiplied glory the

kingdom of David at Jerusalem, to reign over Israel. That is the theme of Isaiah, Jeremiah, Ezekiel, Micah, Zechariah and other prophets.

The Rod From the Stem of Jesse

In Isaiah 11:1–12 the restoration of David's kingdom is foretold.

"And there shall come forth a rod out of the stem of Jesse, and a Branch shall grow out of his roots: 2 And the spirit of the Lord shall rest upon him, the spirit of wisdom and understanding, the spirit of counsel and might, the spirit of knowledge and of the fear of the Lord; 3 And shall make him of quick understanding in the fear of the Lord: and he shall not judge after the sight of his eyes, neither reprove after the hearing of his ears: 4 But with righteousness shall he judge the poor, and reprove with equity for the meek of the earth: and he shall smite the earth with the rod of his mouth, and with the breath of his lips shall he slay the wicked. 5 And righteousness shall be the girdle of his loins, and faithfulness the girdle of his reins. 6 The wolf also shall dwell with the lamb, and the leopard shall lie down with the kid; and the calf and the young lion and the fatling together; and a little child shall lead them. 7 And the cow and the bear shall feed; their young ones shall lie down together: and the lion shall eat straw like the ox. 8 And the sucking child shall play on the hole of the asp, and the weaned child shall put his hand on the cockatrice' den. 9 They shall not hurt nor destroy in all my holy mountain: for the earth shall be full of the knowledge of the Lord, as the waters cover the sea. 10 And in that day there shall be a root of Jesse, which shall stand for an ensign of the people; to it shall the Gentiles seek: and his rest shall be glorious. 11 And it shall come to pass in that day, that the Lord shall set his hand again the second time to recover the remnant of his people, which shall be left, from Assyria, and from Egypt, and from Pathros, and from Cush, and from Elam, and from Shinar, and from Hamath, and from the islands of the sea. 12 And he shall set up an ensign for the nations, and shall assemble the outcasts of Israel, and gather together the dispersed of Judah from the four corners of the earth."
—Isaiah 11:1–12.

Jesse was the father of David, and verse 1 means that from the "stem" or trunk of David's line, a Rod or a Sprout should grow to restore David's kingdom. "A Branch shall grow out of his roots." In the New Testament it is made clear that Jesus is the Son of David. Ot that we will learn more later. But in this passage, Isaiah shows that the coming Saviour would restore the kingdom of David on earth.

Not Fulfilled at Christ's First Coming

If you read the passage you cannot help seeing that this did not occur at the first coming of Christ, and has not yet occurred. Verse 4 says that He shall "smite the earth with the rod of his mouth and with the breath of his lips shall he slay the wicked."

But Jesus did not slay the wicked. Nor does the gospel slay the wicked nor smite the earth today. This verse could not mean that Christ through the gospel ever smites the earth with various catastrophes and plagues, for that would be just as true of preceding centuries as during the present time. The poor are not judged in righteousness and the meek do not have their enemies reproved now, as verse 4 says they will have. That would be a mere "private interpretation" of Scripture, which is forbidden in the Scriptures (II Pet. 1:20), to explain away the plain intent of this passage, count it all figurative language, and so dismiss it.

Study verses 6 to 8. The nature of wild animals has not been changed yet as is pictured in this passage. Lions do not now eat straw like oxen, a sucking child cannot safely play on the hole of the asp (one of the most poisonous of snakes), nor put his hand on the cockatrice' den. Calves and lions and cows and bears do not lie down together nor feed together. Jesus did not change the nature of wild animals at His first coming, and the gospel has not done it yet.

This Teaching, the Branch of David to Rule Over Israel, Repeated Several Times

Jeremiah was inspired to tell the same story and we find it clearly stated in two passages.

"And I will gather the remnant of my flock out of all countries whither I have driven them, and will bring them again to their folds; and they shall be fruitful and increase. And I will set up

shepherds over them which shall feed them: and they shall fear no more, nor be dismayed, neither shall they be lacking, saith the Lord. Behold, the days come, saith the Lord, that I will raise unto David a righteous BRANCH, and a King shall reign and prosper, and shall execute judgment and justice in the earth. In his days Judah shall be saved, and Israel shall dwell safely: and this is his name whereby he shall be called, THE LORD OUR RIGHT-EOUSNESS."—Jer. 23:3–6.

"Behold, the days come, saith the Lord, that I will perform that good thing which I have promised unto the house of Israel and to the house of Judah. In those days, and at that time, will I cause the BRANCH of righteousness to grow up unto David; and he shall execute judgment and righteousness in the land. In those days shall Judah be saved, and Jerusalem shall dwell safely: and this is the name wherewith she shall be called, The Lord our righteousness. For thus saith the Lord; David shall never want a man to sit upon the throne of the house of Israel."—Jer. 33:14–17.

These passages tell of the righteous Branch of David, that He will be a King who "shall reign and prosper, and shall execute judgment and justice IN THE EARTH." In these passages we are plainly told that that seed of David shall be called "the Lord our righteousness," really the Lord Jesus Christ, our present Saviour and our coming King. The regathering, yes, and the salvation of Israel is mentioned here again in connection with the kingdom of this Branch of David's tree, once cut down, but to be restored again with greater glory under David's greater Son.

These passages discuss a kingdom, a reign "in the earth." This is not in Heaven. The throne is not in Heaven, nor is the reign in Heaven. But this King shall reign and prosper and execute judgment and justice—in the earth, Jeremiah 23:5 says, and "in the land," Jeremiah 33:15 says. This is the same reign about which Isaiah 11 tells us when the nature of the wild animals shall be changed and the knowledge of the Lord shall cover the earth.

We may take it, then, as a well-defined doctrine in the Old Testament that there must appear a great Descendant of David who will reign on David's throne at Jerusalem and that the monarchy of David in Palestine will be restored again in an everlasting kingdom on the earth.

The Throne of David, the Nation Israel, the Land of Canaan

In this chapter and the two preceding chapters, you have been impressed, I trust, with the truth that all the unfulfilled promises and prophecies of the Bible center around one land, one race and one throne. These three, the throne of David, over the people Israel, in the land of Canaan, form the triple center of all prophecy. One who understands God's covenant with Abraham about the land Canaan, His covenant with Israel about their restoration and conversion, and the covenant with David about his throne, has the heart and center of the prophecies. Almost as prominent in the prophecies as these three is the city Jerusalem. The wonderful promises to the holy city are dealt with more fully in chapter nine.

Meanwhile, in chapter six, we will see that Jesus is to be the Branch out of the root of Jesse, "the King of the Jews" who shall reign on David's throne over the whole earth.

Chapter 6

Jesus to Be King of the Jews on David's Throne

AVID'S THRONE is to be established forever as we have learned in the last chapter. Isaiah and Jeremiah told us about that Branch from the root of David that would restore his throne. No one can dispute that Jesus Christ Himself is that Son of David who will sit on David's throne and restore again the kingdom to Israel.

There are many Scriptures that mention this Sprout from the roots or stump of David.

In Revelation 5:5 Jesus is called "the Lion of the tribe of Juda, the Root of David," and in Revelation 22:16, Jesus Himself says, "I am the root and the offspring of David"!

Jesus to Inherit David's Throne

Any Christian could not read far in the Old Testament Scriptures without learning that the Lord Jesus Christ is the Seed of David so many times referred to, the righteous Branch that will restore his kingdom, the King who shall reign and prosper. But in the New Testament this is positively stated again and again. When Mary, an innocent Judean virgin, was visited by the angel Gabriel to announce to her that she should become the mother of the Son of God, she was plainly told that Jesus was to rule on the throne of David. Read Luke 1:30–33 and see how definitely and explicitly the literal reign of Christ on earth was foretold.

"And the angel said unto her, Fear not, Mary: for thou hast found favor with God. And, behold, thou shalt conceive in thy womb, and bring forth a son, and shalt call his name JESUS. He

*shall be great, and shall be called the Son of the Highest: and the
Lord God shall give unto him the throne of his father David:
And he shall reign over the house of Jacob for ever; and of his
kingdom there shall be no end."*

Notice these statements in this Scripture.

"The Lord God shall give unto him the throne of his father
David."

"He shall reign over the house of Jacob for ever."

"Of his kingdom there shall be no end."

The genealogy of Jesus as given through Mary and her father
Heli (Luke 3:23–38; Joseph, not the real father of Jesus, was son-
in-law of Heli) and as given through Joseph (Matt. 1:1–17) both
show that Jesus was literally the Son of David and legally the Son
of David. Fourteen times in the gospels Jesus is called the Son of
David. Therefore Gabriel promised Mary that "God shall give
unto him the throne of his father David: and he shall reign over
the house of Jacob for ever."

The very words of the Scripture in the original manuscripts
are inspired, and how delicate and exact are the meanings of the
words in the Bible! For instances, Jacob had two names, Jacob
and Israel. "Jacob" was the natural man, a schemer, a trickster,
a trader, the thief of his brother's blessing, the deceiver of his father, the scheming son-in-law of Laban. "Israel" was the spiritual
name given to the same man when in all night wrestling with the
angel of God he learned to prevail and become a prince with God
and man. "Israel" was the man of God, the man of prayer, the
victorious Christian. Sometimes Christians like to spiritualize the
name Israel and say that all the children of God are spiritual Israelites. But the Scripture here does not say that Christ is to reign
over "Israel" but over "Jacob," that is, over literal flesh and blood
Jews, the literal, physical descendants of Abraham, the same race
over whom David reigned. Had we been told that Christ should
reign over "Israel," men would have been quick to say that it
meant a spiritual reign in the hearts of Christians. But the Lord
caused the angel to use the specific word "Jacob," and the Holy
Spirit inspired Luke to write it down so that we might know that
the kingdom of Christ on earth will be a literal Jewish kingdom
over the house of Jacob on the literal throne of David!

Christ, Like Solomon, to Sit on the Throne of
'Their Father David'

The Scripture tells us that Solomon sat upon the throne of David his father, and the Scripture also tells us that God will give to Christ the throne of His father David. A comparison of these statements in the language of the Bible itself ought to help you to see that Christ will inherit the literal throne of David and will sit upon it literally as Solomon did. For instance, here are some statements of the Scriptures:

"Then sat Solomon upon the THRONE OF DAVID HIS FA-THER; and his kingdom was established greatly."—I Kings 2:12.

"He shall be great, and shall be called the Son of the Highest: and the Lord God shall give unto him THE THRONE OF HIS FATHER DAVID: And he shall reign over the house of Jacob for ever; and of his kingdom there shall be no end."

—Luke 1:32, 33.

The first verse is about Solomon, and the second about Jesus. Solomon sat upon the throne of his father David. The angel said to Mary that the Lord God would give to Jesus the throne of His Father David. If the Bible meant a literal reign in the first case, then why should it not mean a literal reign in the second case? Any honest interpretation of the Scripture must lead us to the conclusion that the reign of Christ will be on the literal throne of David at Jerusalem, where Solomon reigned.

The Genealogy of Jesus

The genealogies of Jesus given by the Holy Spirit to Matthew and Luke particularly prove that Christ is the promised Son of David. That genealogy given in Matthew begins with this statement: "The book of the generation of Jesus Christ, the son of David, the son of Abraham" (Matt. 1:1).

Two important points the Holy Spirit makes with regard to this genealogy. First, Christ is the promised Son of David who will sit upon David's throne and rule as King of the Jews. Second, Jesus is the Son of Abraham. This means that Christ is the "seed" of Abraham mentioned in the Abrahamic Covenant (Gen. 13:15; Gen. 17:7–8). The Holy Spirit calls attention in Galatians 3:16

to the fact that the seed is singular, referring to Christ. Christ is THE Son of David. So He is "THE Son of Abraham," and not just one descendant of Abraham. In other words, Christ is the promised King and He is the promised Heir of the land of Canaan with Abraham.

It is an interesting fact that the genealogy given in Matthew is only the official genealogy, not the actual one. The account given in Matthew 1:1–16 ends with the statement: "And Jacob begat Joseph the husband of Mary, of whom was born Jesus, who is called Christ." (v. 16). The genealogy given is that of Joseph, the husband of Mary. Then the remainder of the chapter tells how Mary "was found with child of the Holy Ghost" "before they came together." Joseph was not the father of Jesus, and the genealogy given is a legal one, but not the actual one.

Now compare with this the genealogy found in Luke 3:23–38 which genealogy starts off with the following words: "And Jesus himself began to be about thirty years of age, being (as was supposed) the son of Joseph, which was *the son* of Heli." Matthew 1:16 says that "Jacob begat Joseph the husband of Mary," while Luke 3:23 says, "Joseph which was *the son* of Heli." Who was the father of Joseph, was it Jacob or Heli? It was Jacob because we are plainly told that "Jacob begat Joseph." Then who was Heli? *Heli was the father of Mary, and Joseph was the son-in-law of Heli.* It would be in accordance with Jewish custom to call him the son of Heli, but actually the words "the son" were not in the original Greek, but were supplied by the translators, which they indicated by putting the words in italics. In Luke, then, we have actually the genealogy of Jesus the Son of David and King of the Jews.

Another remarkable difference is shown in these two genealogies. One is giving the ancestry of Joseph back to David, and the other the ancestry of Mary and of Jesus back to David. Joseph's line descended from Solomon, David's son, while Jesus, through Mary, actually descended from David through another son, Nathan. Joseph, the foster father of Jesus, was a descendant of the last king that sat on David's throne before the captivity (Matt. 1:11). Consider Jechonias, mentioned in Matthew 1:11. He is also called Jehoiachin, Jeconiah and Coniah in various places in the Scriptures. Matthew says that Joseph, the husband of Mary, was descended from this Jechonias or Coniah. But Jeremiah 22:30 says of this man that he should be written childless, for none of his seed should ever prosper on the throne of David! What a wonderful example this is of the inspiration of the Scriptures. Joseph could not have been the father of Jesus, and Jesus could not have counted His ancestry through the last of the reigning kings of Judah, according to divine Writ. Instead, the literal genealogy of Jesus tells us in Luke 3:31, that He was "of Nathan, which was the son of David."

Do not confuse these genealogies nor think them the same; they are not. The two genealogies sometimes have similar names, but they are not names of the same people. The lines diverge at David and come back at Joseph and Mary to prove Jesus the legal and actual Son of David and the Heir of David's throne.

Wise Men Sought "the King of the Jews"

Those wise men who came from the East to find the Saviour at His birth inquired saying: "Where is he that is born King of the Jews? for we have seen his star in the east, and are come to worship him" (Matt. 2:2). How did these wise men learn about the coming Saviour? They could have learned in only two ways: either they read the prophecies of the Old Testament and understood that Jesus would be the King of the Jews, or they had it revealed to them directly from God. I think they learned it both ways. They were Magi, that is wise men, from the East, most probably from Babylon, since that was the first great nation eastward. And we know from the book of Daniel that a class of great men were there called by such a name. Daniel, remember, had been the greatest man in Babylon, next to the king himself, through a long period of years and through the reign of several world rulers. His religion and his writings could hardly have been a secret to the scholars of great Babylon. From Daniel 9:25, they doubtless learned the approximate time of the Saviour's first coming so plainly foretold there. God probably revealed to them through the Holy Spirit something about the nature of this coming Saviour, and gave the star in the East as a sign of the birth of the Child.

We come to the inescapable conclusion that a careful study of the Old Testament by spiritually-minded men led them to understand that the Saviour would be the King of the Jews. The leading of the Holy Spirit confirmed their honest belief. The wise men were right. Jesus is to be the King of the Jews and rule in a Jewish kingdom on this earth.

When we read more of the story in Matthew 2:3-6, we see that Herod expected the Saviour to rule literally in the land of Palestine, over Jews. His jealousy and fear for his own kingdom led to the murder of all the boy babies who might, he thought, fulfill the promise of God about the kingdom of the Jews.

Read Matthew 2:3-6:

"When Herod the king had heard these things, he was troubled, and all Jerusalem with him. And when he had gathered all the chief priests and scribes of the people together, he demanded of them where Christ should be born. And they said unto him, In Bethlehem of Judaea: for thus it is written by the prophet, And thou Bethlehem, in the land of Juda, art not the least among the princes of Juda: for out of thee shall come a Governor, that shall rule my people Israel."

Here we see that "all the chief priests and scribes of the people" agreed with Herod that the coming Saviour would be primarily a King, a Prince of Judah, "a Governor, that shall rule my people Israel." They proved it by quoting from Micah 5:2!

This attitude of all the people expecting Christ to take the literal throne of David and rule in Palestine from Jerusalem over a literal kingdom is shown throughout the Bible. There is not a single indication that any Jew or Christian Gentile in either the Old or New Testament believed otherwise. There were no postmillennialists in Bible times. Every Jew, including the twelve apostles, expected the kingdom of Christ to be literal and that the Saviour should sit on the throne of David. Jesus did not one time rebuke this thought!

Christ Presented as King of the Jews

When John the Baptist came as the forerunner of Christ and to announce His ministry, he came preaching, "Repent ye: for the kingdom of heaven is at hand" (Matt. 3:2). What did he mean? Surely he must have meant the kingdom which was long foretold in the Old Testament. In fact, the term "the kingdom of heaven" probably was taken from Daniel 2:44 where we are told that "the God of heaven" shall "set up a kingdom, which shall never be destroyed." John was speaking, evidently, about the kingdom which the God of Heaven would set up, and therefore called it the kingdom of Heaven. A heavenly kingdom on this earth, according to John the Baptist, was at hand. This term "the kingdom of heaven" is used only in the Gospel of Matthew, though the same kingdom is mentioned in many, many other places in the Bible.

Jesus preached the same kind of sermons exactly, in the beginning of His ministry, for Matthew 4:17 tells us: "From that time Jesus began to preach, and to say, Repent: for the kingdom of heaven is at hand." Just a little later, still in the early part of His ministry, Jesus sent out His twelve apostles as forerunners, not to Gentiles nor Samaritans, and Matthew 10:6–7 tells us that He instructed them: "But go rather to the lost sheep of the house of Israel. And as ye go, preach, saying, The kingdom of heaven is at hand."

At Hand! What Did Jesus Mean?

John the Baptist and the twelve apostles all preached to the Jews, at the beginning of Christ's ministry, that the kingdom of Heaven was "at hand." Did that mean it had begun? Did that mean the kingdom would begin unconditionally at some set time, in the immediate future? No, by the exhortation, "Repent: for the kingdom of heaven is at hand," Jesus and His representatives certainly meant that the kingdom of Heaven was now possible and near, in the presence of the King Himself, and that the establishment of that kingdom depended on repentance by the Jewish nation. The kingdom was not "IN hand," it was "AT hand." The term used simply means nigh or near. The kingdom had not begun. If the Jews had repented and accepted Christ as their Saviour and King, then the kingdom would soon have been restored to Israel.

In fact, Christ's coming as Saviour to an individual and as Saviour and King to the Jewish nation are on the same basis. Christ is nigh unto all who call upon Him for salvation. He is "at hand" for every sinner who wants to be saved. That was true then, and is true now about salvation. But concerning the kingdom of Heaven, there is a difference. That kingdom was at hand at the beginning of Christ's ministry, but after the rejection of Christ as Saviour and King became persistent, malicious and national in scope, then the kingdom was no longer at hand. Any Jew may trust Christ as Saviour today, for as a Saviour He is still at hand. But Jews cannot have their kingdom until the King returns. Christ can save sinners through the gospel and through the Holy Spirit, and those who are saved are "born of the Spirit" (John 3:6), but Christ cannot reign over Israel in the spirit but must sit in the flesh on the throne of David; for that throne was a literal, physical throne. The kingdom was postponed until the King returns.

Christ Rejected as King

The national leaders of Israel, the scribes and Pharisees and elders, were first greatly impressed with the preaching of John the Baptist; and many of them went to be baptized by him in the River Jordan. But they were a self-righteous group and had utterly ignored the command to repent.

John the Baptist called them a "generation of vipers," or snakes, and warned them of the fires of Hell (Matt. 3:7-12). These religious leaders were willing to have a king if that did not involve repentance and a change of heart. Actually they were ungodly and wicked; they were Jews outwardly but not inwardly. When Jesus pressed continually the command to repent and denounced their hypocrisy, they began to hate Him. It soon became evident that the rejection of Christ as Saviour and King of Israel was deliberate and national. The last time Jesus had it preached that "the kingdom of heaven is at hand" was in the tenth chapter of Matthew. In the next chapter (Matt. 11:20) we are told: "Then began he to upbraid the cities wherein most of his mighty works were done, because they repented not." Chorazin, Bethsaida, and Capernaum are particularly named as under condemnation for their sins more than Tyre, Sidon, and Sodom, since the latter cities would have repented at the preaching they heard. After this you will find in the ministry of Jesus that His message is not about a kingdom then at hand, for the people refused to repent and the kingdom was postponed.

Some of the common people, without any sincere repentance,

would have gladly made Jesus King even by violence, because of His miraculous feeding of the five thousand (John 6:14, 15). He Himself said that "the kingdom of heaven suffereth violence, and the violent take it by force" (Matt. 11:12. See also Luke 16:16). But as He continued preaching about repentance and being born again, and about His own crucifixion, the Jewish people as a whole, as unspiritual as their leaders, were offended at His preaching and left Him to follow Him no more. "From that time many of his disciples went back, and walked no more with him" (John 6:66). In John 7:1 we are told that Jesus would not walk in Jewry, that is, among the Jews, "because the Jews sought to kill him."

The die is now cast; the Jews have rejected their King, and the story moves on, in the gospels, to the crucifixion.

Christ Crucified as King of the Jews

Christ died for the sins of the world, and we know that God had in mind salvation of sinners when He allowed His dear Son to be crucified. "God so loved the world" that Jesus went to the cross. The plan of Jesus was the same as the plan of the Father. It was no accident when Jesus was crucified. Men did not thwart the plan of God. Christ did not die as a martyr. He Himself said concerning His death:

"Therefore doth my Father love me, because I lay down my life, that I might take it again. No man taketh it from me, but I lay it down of myself. I have power to lay it down, and I have power to take it again. This commandment have I received of my Father" (John 10:17, 18).

Christ died as our passover Lamb (I Cor. 5:7). "All we like sheep have gone astray; we have turned every one to his own way; and the Lord hath laid on him the iniquity of us all" (Isa. 53:6). In the mind and plan of God, Christ died in our stead and to be our Saviour.

But this was not the plan of the Jewish rulers. They hated Jesus because He claimed the right to be King. They accused Him to Pilate and sought His crucifixion on the ground that He claimed to be the King of the Jews. Luke 23:1-3 says:

*"And the whole multitude of them arose, and led him unto
Pilate. And they began to accuse him, saying, We found this fel-
low perverting the nation, and forbidding to give tribute to Caesar, saying that he himself is Christ a King. And Pilate asked him,
saying, Art thou the King of the Jews? And he answered him and
said, Thou sayest it."*

When Pilate wrote over the head of Jesus, "This is Jesus of
Nazareth, the King of the Jews," these wicked enemies of Christ
urged Pilate to change the accusation and make it read that Jesus
said He was the King of the Jews. But Pilate refused. Christ was
crucified as King of the Jews and the crucifixion from their view-
point was simply a concrete evidence of their refusal to repent
and of their rejection of Him as King. The people said to Pilate,
"We have no king but Caesar" (John 19:15).

So the Jews rejected their King and the kingdom was postponed.

Does that seem unreasonable to you? Then remember that the
same plan obtains in the case of practically every sinner. Christ is
offered as Saviour to every man just as He was offered to the Jews.
Do you object to the thought that Jews could reject their King,
and the kingdom would be postponed and later set up? Then remember that many a sinner has first rejected Christ, again and
again, and then later has received Him as Saviour and Lord. We
may safely say that God is willing to save today every sinner who
will repent, for the Scripture says that He is "not willing that any
should perish, but that all should come to repentance" (II Pet.
3:9). But sinners rejected the plan of God as did these Jews.

Many times individual sinners reject Christ too long and so are
lost forever. The same thing was true of many individual Jews in
the time of Christ, for God has not foretold in the Scriptures that
He will save some particular individual. He will save all who put
their trust in Him, but individuals may or may not be saved.
However, with the nation Israel it is different, for God has plainly
promised that Christ shall have His kingdom, and have it He
will, when His time comes. But it will be offered them on the
basis of repentance; and Israel will repent and be converted, as
they ought to have done before.

The Church Age, a Mystery Hid in Ages Past

God knew, of course, that Jews would reject their Saviour and King, just as He knows what every sinner will do about the gospel when it is preached to him, just as He knows all things. But that Israel might have the entire responsibility of accepting or rejecting the King of the Jews, most of the events of this present church or gospel age were not made known in the Old Testament times. The prophet Joel foretold the pouring out of the Holy Spirit, but aside from that the prophets of the Old Testament seem not to have had any revelation at all of this entire period of time from Pentecost on through the present to the second coming of Christ. Jesus Himself did not give revelations concerning the course of this age with its rejection of the gospel, its wars, wickedness, and the worldliness of professing Christians, until after He ceased to preach that the kingdom of Heaven is at hand. To Paul the apostle was first given an understanding of some of the mysteries concerning the church in this age. Ephesians 3:1–10 tells us how Paul was given this grace to understand and teach how that Gentiles would be in the same body with Jews, the church. And Ephesians 3:5 expressly says that this mystery was not made known in other ages. Search all through the Old Testament and you will not find a single reference to the rapture of the saints.

Much is taught in the Old Testament about the second coming of Christ. But mark this, there is no way to tell, from reading the Old Testament alone, that the first and second comings would not all be the same. Part of the prophecies about Christ's coming were fulfilled at His first coming. Even more of them are yet to be fulfilled and will be fulfilled at His Second Coming. He has already come as the Lamb of God, but He has not come as the Lion of the Tribe of Judah. He has already come as the Man of sorrows, rejected, despised, and bruised for our iniquities, as foretold in the fifty-third chapter of Isaiah. But His coming to rule on David's throne, to execute justice on the earth, and with the breath of His lips to slay the wicked, as foretold in the eleventh chapter of Isaiah, has not been fulfilled. The mystery of this present church age coming between the first and second comings of Christ was hidden from the Old Testament prophets. God knew that the Jews would reject their King, but He left the responsibility upon them and did not reveal it until it had come to pass and the kingdom was postponed.

This will help you to understand why the prophets of the Old Testament looked forward always to the coming kingdom; and why, in the New Testament Epistles, Christians are again and again exhorted to look forward to the rapture of the saints, before the kingdom, while in the gospels Jesus spoke primarily to Jews and so spoke much about the kingdom but also referred to the rapture (for example, in the parable of the ten virgins, Matthew 25:1–13).

Chapter 7

The Kingdom Postponed Until the King Returns

*A*FTER THE rejection of Christ by the Jews was general and national, then Jesus taught often about the kingdom and always made clear that it was now postponed. In introducing the parable of the pounds (Luke 19:11–27), Luke tells us that He spake this parable to them because they thought that the kingdom of God should immediately appear. So He corrected their false impression and told them that He would be like a nobleman who should go into a far country and receive a kingdom, and then return to reign; that He would then allow faithful servants to rule with Him and would punish His enemies. Then in the parable Jesus referred to the Jews who had rejected Him saying, "But his citizens hated him, and sent a message after him, saying, We will not have this man to reign over us" (Luke 19:14). The clear teaching of the parable is that when Jesus came the first time, He did not receive the kingdom, but will go to a far country (to Heaven with the Father) until the Father gives Him the kingdom and then will return here to reign.

Jesus gave a similar teaching in the parable of the talents in Matthew 25:14–30. Jesus again illustrates Himself as "a man travelling into a far country" (verse 14). After giving out talents to His servants, Jesus referred to His Second Coming like this: "After a long time the lord of those servants cometh, and reckoneth with them" (verse 19). Again to the faithful servants He said, "I will make thee ruler over many things" (verses 21, 23). Notice the ruling takes place after the Second Coming. In verse 27 Jesus illustrates Himself as coming into His own possessions at His Second Coming, saying, "And then at my coming I should have received mine own with usury." Then in the first verse after this parable, Jesus says in Matthew 25:31: "When the Son of man shall come in his glory, and all the holy angels with him, THEN shall he sit upon the throne of his glory."

Jesus is clearly teaching that now His kingdom is postponed and that He will not reign until He comes back, like the man who is gone into a far country. But when He returns and all the holy angels with Him, "THEN shall he sit upon the throne of his glory," and His faithful servants that have done well during this church or gospel age will then be appointed by Him to rule with Him over many things.

"But Now Is My Kingdom Not From Hence"

When Jesus stood before Pilate, He gave this same teaching that His kingdom was postponed. Pilate said to Jesus, "Art thou the King of the Jews?" and "What hast thou done?" (John 18:33, 35). The Holy Spirit tells us the clear answer of Jesus in John 18:36: "Jesus answered, My kingdom is not of this world: if my kingdom were of this world, then would my servants fight, that I should not be delivered to the Jews: but now is my kingdom not from hence." The word "world" used here means the present order or arrangement, the present system. Jesus said, "My kingdom is not of this world," that is, not of the present system. And then He explained more fully "now is my kingdom not from hence." 'My kingdom, rejected by the Jews, now will not come at this time and will not be of this present world order,' said Jesus in effect. The kingdom of Christ will not come until the end of this present world order. The present "world" (the Greek word is *kosmos*) will end at the return of Christ when present civilization and governments will be utterly destroyed. Then Christ will have His kingdom.

At the last supper with His disciples before the crucifixion, Jesus comforted the hearts of His disciples concerning His kingdom and promised them that they should eat and drink at His table in that kingdom and sit on thrones judging the twelve tribes of Israel. In Luke 22:28–30 Jesus said:

"Ye are they which have continued with me in my temptations. And I appoint unto you a kingdom, as my Father hath appointed

unto me; That ye may eat and drink at my table in my kingdom, and sit on thrones judging the twelve tribes of Israel."

The postponed kingdom of Jesus is not of this world, that is, not of this present order of things. In Matthew 19:28 Jesus gave a similar promise to His disciples and said they should reign with Him on twelve thrones "when the Son of man shall sit in the throne of his glory."

John the Baptist, Jesus, and His apostles preached, "Repent ye: for the kingdom of heaven is at hand" (Matt. 3:2; Matt. 4:17; Matt. 10:7). Jews, as a nation, were addressed in these first messages, and enormous throngs representing the entire nation listened to these sermons. However, the nation did not repent and accept the King and His kingdom; so soon the character of the message was changed. Jesus and the apostles still preached the gospel, the "good news." But it was good news of salvation at hand, not any longer good news about a kingdom at hand. He called out individuals, saying, "Come unto me, all ye that labour and are heavy laden, and I will give you rest" (Matt. 11:28). He still commanded people to repent (Luke 13:3, 5), but He did not say, "for the kingdom of heaven is at hand."

John the Baptist, Jesus, and His apostles preached, "Repent: for the kingdom of heaven is at hand." Peter, after the wonderful outpouring of the Spirit at Pentecost, again addressed the Jewish leaders and preached to representatives of the whole nation and said, "Repent ye therefore." He did not say in that passage that the kingdom of Heaven was at hand as it had been before the Jewish leaders and people rejected Christ and refused to repent. Instead He plainly tells them that they should now repent, not expecting the IMMEDIATE setting up of the kingdom and that their national sins should be IMMEDIATELY blotted out, but the sins of Israel as a nation should be blotted out AT THE RETURN OF CHRIST! Read Peter's exhortation and see how different it is from the early teaching of John the Baptist and Jesus, that the people should repent to obtain the kingdom which was at hand.

Acts 3:19-21 says:

"Repent ye therefore, and be converted, that your sins may be blotted out, when the times of refreshing shall come from the

presence of the Lord; And he shall send Jesus Christ, which before was preached unto you: Whom the heaven must receive until the times of restitution of all things, which God hath spoken by the mouth of all his holy prophets since the world began."

Of course, we know that an individual's sins are blotted out when he believes in Christ (John 3:18), but the sins of Israel as a nation will not be blotted out until "the times of refreshing" when God "shall send Jesus Christ" to the earth again "whom the heaven must receive until the times of restitution." Then, in that time of refreshing and restitution of the things promised by the prophets, the throne of David will be restored, Israel will be restored and their sins as a nation will be blotted out from the sight of God, and they will be no more punished.

The Apostles Preached Repentance and the Kingdom, But Never That the Kingdom Was at Hand

After Israel rejected their King and refused to qualify nationally for the restoration of the kingdom to Israel, the command to repent was not withdrawn. Jesus commanded the apostles that repentance and forgiveness of sins should be preached in all nations (Luke 24:47). Paul preached that God has COMMANDED ALL MEN EVERY WHERE to repent (Acts 17:30). In II Peter 3:9 we are told that God would have ALL come to repentance. But notice this fact: NOT ONCE, AFTER THE REJECTION OF CHRIST BY THE JEWISH OFFICIALS AND THE MULTITUDES, DID ANY BIBLE PREACHER TEACH THAT "THE KINGDOM OF HEAVEN IS AT HAND"! The kingdom was no longer at hand but was postponed.

The story of the kingdom was called "the gospel," that is, good news or tidings, while the kingdom was said to be at hand. Jesus preached "the gospel of the kingdom" (Matt. 4:23; Matt. 9:35) as long as the kingdom was at hand. After that He taught concerning the kingdom and preached the gospel or good news of salvation, but a postponed kingdom was not good news and that part was not called the gospel. All of the apostles preached concerning the kingdom of God and kingdom of Heaven, but the Bible never says that any of them, after the early ministry of Christ, preached "the gospel of the kingdom."

However, the gospel of the kingdom is to be preached again during the tribulation period and just before Christ returns to set up His kingdom. In Matthew 24 Jesus was teaching His disciples and us about the things surrounding His coming and the end of the world (verse 3). Verse 8 in that chapter tells of "the beginning of sorrows." Verse 15 tells of "the abomination of desolation, spoken of by Daniel the prophet" in Daniel 9:27, which will happen in the midst of the seven years of trouble which precede the reign of Christ on earth. Understand; the coming of Jesus into the air to receive His saints will evidently be at the first of the seven years, before the Man of Sin is revealed (II Thess. 2:6, 8), but His return with His saints to reign cannot come until the close of the seven years. Then (still in Matthew 24), verse 21 plainly says that the time discussed is the Great Tribulation, and verses 29 and 30 say that IMMEDIATELY AFTER THE TRIBULATION ALL THE TRIBES OF THE EARTH SHALL SEE THE SON OF MAN COMING IN THE CLOUDS OF HEAVEN.

So you see clearly when you read Matthew 24 carefully that the discussion is about the last days just before Christ returns visibly and bodily to the earth. Now here is an interesting fact; IN THOSE DAYS OF THE GREAT TRIBULATION, THE GOSPEL OF THE KINGDOM WILL BE PREACHED AGAIN! For in the same chapter, Matthew 24:14 tells us, "And this gospel of the kingdom shall be preached in all the world for a witness unto all nations; and then shall the end come." Again the kingdom of Heaven will be "at hand," impending, drawing nigh, and it will be good news to troubled Jews and all Christians who have prayed, "Thy kingdom come. Thy will be done in earth, as it is in heaven."

Chapter 8

The Kingdom of Christ on Earth Is Yet Future

ESUS IS GOD, and in some sense has part in all the rule of God the Father over this universe. We are clearly told that Christ is now sitting on the right hand of the Father in His throne (Rev. 3:21; Eph. 1:20), and before giving the Great Commission, Jesus Himself said, "All power is given unto me in heaven and in earth." When we talk about the reign of Christ on David's throne, we do not mean that Jesus is not now God, possessing all the kingly attributes of God. But David's throne and God's throne in Heaven are entirely different thrones. God was on His throne in Heaven before David was given a throne at Jerusalem. When David ruled at Jerusalem, the throne in Heaven was unchanged and its glory was undiminished. When David's throne was temporarily vacated and the children of Israel carried into captivity, there was no change in the throne of God in Heaven. As far as the Scriptures reveal, there has been no change in the throne of God in Heaven through all the centuries of human existence. Its glory had not been diminished and it could not be increased. Christ now shares the glory that He had with the Father in the beginning and no Christian can deny that Jesus is now Lord as well as Christ. Jesus now has authority with the Father just as He shares the nature of the Father.

But the reign of Christ on the throne of David is not the same as the reign of the Father in Heaven. David's throne belongs to God, is subject to the heavenly throne, but David's throne is not the heavenly throne. The throne of God in Heaven has always been established. But the reign or kingdom of Christ on David's throne is yet future.

Jesus Taught Us to Pray for His Future Kingdom

The Bible is full of proof that the kingdom of Christ is not yet set up and that Christ is not now on His Throne. In the model prayer Jesus taught us how to pray, in these dear and familiar words: "Our Father which art in heaven, Hallowed be thy name. Thy kingdom come. Thy will be done in earth, as it is in heaven" (Matt. 6:9–10). Jesus wants us to pray "Thy kingdom come"! The kingdom had not come when Jesus gave the command to pray this prayer. Notice that to the first three petitions of the 'Lord's Prayer' there can be but one answer. The name of God is not hallowed in this world now. His will is not done on earth as the angels perfectly obey Him in Heaven. These other two petitions must be answered when the kingdom comes. When Christ rules on this earth in a literal kingdom, then the name of God will be kept sacred and without blasphemy. Then God's will shall be done on earth. It is not so now. This prayer clearly shows us that the kingdom of Christ is in the future.

How far Christians have missed the spirit of this prayer! The first thought of a Christian when he prays should be to long for the coming of the Saviour, His kingdom, and the time when man shall reverence God's name and do His will on the earth as it is done in Heaven. The second coming of Christ is as central, as emphatic, and as pervasive in the teaching of the Bible as is His first coming. The Second Coming is the Christian's "blessed hope" (Titus 2:13), his constant watch (Mark 13:33–37), and, according to the model prayer, it should be his daily prayer. The millions who daily pray, "Thy kingdom come," are praying, whether they know it or not, for the return of Jesus and the setting up of His reign on the earth.

The Bible Constantly Mentions the Kingdom as Future

Jesus never left a doubt with His disciples that His kingdom was in the future. In Matthew 19:28, 29 He said unto His disciples:

"Verily I say unto you, That ye which have followed me, in the regeneration when the Son of man shall sit in the throne of his glory, ye also shall sit upon twelve thrones, judging the twelve

tribes of Israel. And every one that hath forsaken houses, or brethren, or sisters, or father, or mother, or wife, or children, or lands, for my name's sake, shall receive an hundredfold, and shall inherit everlasting life."

When Jesus spoke these words, He did not sit "in the throne of his glory." He referred to a future time "in the regeneration," that is, when things are made new, when the Son of man should sit on the throne of His glory. At that time the twelve apostles shall sit on the twelve thrones, He said, judging the twelve tribes of Israel. Jesus is to reign over the house of Jacob, on the throne of His father David (Luke 1:32, 33). His apostles will sit on thrones at the same time to judge the tribes. The wildest stretch of the imagination does not picture apostles now sitting on the thrones, judging the twelve tribes of Israel. It was future when Jesus mentioned it. It is future still.

When Jesus stood before Pilate, charged with claiming to be King of the Jews, He explained to Pilate that His kingdom was not of this present "world" (the Greek word is *kosmos,* meaning the present social and political order, the present civilization). Jesus did not mean that His kingdom would not be on this planet. The kingdom of Christ will be on this earth, but not of this present civilization, this political and social order. Here is what Jesus told Pilate: "My kingdom is not of this world: if my kingdom were of this world, then would my servants fight, that I should not be delivered to the Jews: but now is my kingdom not from hence" (John 18:36).

Pilate understood and believed the claim of Jesus that He would one day rule as King of the Jews, and so the Roman ruler had it put above His head on the cross when Jesus died, "This is Jesus of Nazareth, the King of the Jews." The kingdom of Christ will be on this earth, but not of this present world. No, it must be "in the regeneration" (Matt. 19:28), in the time of "the restitution of all things" (Acts 3:19–21).

"Wilt Thou at This Time Restore Again the Kingdom to Israel?"

After Jesus was risen from the dead, the kingdom was yet future. In Acts 1:6, 7 the disciples raised with Jesus the burning question of the time of His kingdom. They had heard all His teachings. Jesus had opened their hearts after the resurrection to understand the Scriptures (Luke 24:45). Do not mock at their question. I would rather have the theological training of Peter, James, and John, three years of intimate teaching by the Saviour Himself, than to have a degree from all the seminaries in this world. Smart professors often say that the apostles were foolish to expect still an earthly kingdom, but I remind you that Jesus never said so.

Here are the apostles of Jesus, trained, empowered and authorized to carry on His work after His ascension, which is about to take place. Knowing the hundreds of promises about the coming kingdom, the covenants with Abraham, Isaac, Jacob, David, and Israel, their hearts longed for the restoration of the kingdom of David under Jesus, as was revealed in the Old Testament and then promised by the angel to Mary. Let us hear the disciples' question and the answer of Jesus:

"When they therefore were come together, they asked of him, saying, Lord, wilt thou at this time restore again the kingdom to Israel? And he said unto them, It is not for you to know the times or the seasons, which the Father hath put in his own power. But ye shall receive power, after that the Holy Ghost is come upon you: and ye shall be witnesses unto me both in Jerusalem, and in all Judaea, and in Samaria, and unto the uttermost part of the earth."—Acts 1:6–8.

Be sure you understand the question! The disciples did not ask "Lord, wilt thou restore again the kingdom to Israel?" No, no, they knew all too well the promises which made certain the re-establishment of that kingdom under Christ. Their question was altogether about the TIME of restoration of that kingdom. "Lord, wilt thou AT THIS TIME restore again the kingdom to Israel?" they asked. The apostles simply asked to know if it was time for the kingdom to be set up. That is what they asked, and that is what Jesus answered. Jesus did not rebuke them for thinking the kingdom would be restored to Israel. He simply said, "It is not for you to know the times." The kingdom of Christ was not set up when Jesus had finished His earthly ministry, had risen from the dead, and was ready to ascend back to the Father.

The Kingdom Not Established at Pentecost

Notice this other thing, the kingdom was not set up at Pentecost. The pouring out of the Holy Spirit, which Jesus promised should come "not many days hence," was the subject of the discussion when the disciples brought up the question about the time of the restoration of the kingdom to Israel under Christ. Jesus plainly indicated that when He talked about the baptism of the Holy Spirit or the pouring out of the Spirit He was not talking about the kingdom.

Read again Acts 1:6–8 and you will see, if you look closely, that this is true. When the disciples asked if this was the time that the kingdom was to be restored to Israel, Jesus replied that the matter of this kingdom pertained to "the times or the seasons, which the Father hath put in HIS own power," and this, it was not for them to know. Not a word in the Bible has ever made known the time of the coming of Christ and the things that follow it. The bringing of that kingdom God has kept "in his own power." That is, that kingdom will be set up by the power of God, not by any work of men. That is the reason we are told in Daniel 2:44 that in those days "shall the God of heaven set up a kingdom." That kingdom will not be set up by human hands nor by human works but by God Himself. He has kept it "in His own power."

But the matter of winning souls in this gospel age is another matter, and for that God will give men power, the power of the Holy Spirit. That is what Jesus meant in the above passage. Read it again.

"When they therefore were come together, they asked of him, saying, Lord, wilt thou at this time restore again the kingdom to Israel? And he said unto them, It is not for you to know the times or the seasons, which the Father hath put IN HIS OWN POWER. But YE shall receive power, after that the Holy Ghost is come upon you: and ye shall be witnesses unto me both in Jerusalem, and in all Judaea, and in Samaria, and unto the uttermost part of the earth."—Acts 1:6–8.

The power and authority for restoring the kingdom to Israel, when Christ will sit on the throne of David, the Father has kept in His own hands. It is not for us to know the times or seasons concerning that, not even for the apostles to know it. But power for soul winning, He had plainly promised them, should come when they were baptized with the Holy Ghost "not many days hence" (Acts 1:5). Holy Spirit power for soul winning was definitely promised for the immediate future, AND THEY WERE NOT TO LEAVE JERUSALEM UNTIL THEY GOT IT! But the authority and power for restoring the kingdom to Israel the Father has reserved in His own power and it is not for them to know that time.

One of the worst mistakes one can make in the study of prophecy is to try to set the times and seasons which it is not for us to know and which the Father has put in His own power alone. All the Millerites, Seventh Day Adventists, Jehovah's Witnesses, Anglo-Israelites, and others who have attempted to set dates for the Lord's return, have gone wrong because they tried to know the times that are not revealed. Times and seasons pertaining to the restoration of the kingdom to Israel are left in the hands of God. These times and seasons (in other words, these dates) are secret things that belong to God. No chronology in any part of the Bible is given whereby we may set the dates for these things. Those who interpret Daniel or Revelation or any other part of the Bible with a view to making a day mean a year (which it never does mean in the Bible) in order to set the date for the return of Christ, the restoration of the kingdom to Israel, etc., violate the plain teaching of the Word of God. They try to know that about which God plainly said, "It is not for you to know" and which God has kept "in His own power."

Some people say that the kingdom was set up at Pentecost, the restoration of this kingdom to Israel. They make the same mistake exactly as other date-setters. Jesus said that the times and seasons of that kingdom were not for the apostles to know and they did not know. Neither do we know. We know the kingdom will be restored to Israel, but *WHEN* is a matter not revealed.

The reason why the time of the restoration of the kingdom to Israel is not told is that it must follow the return of Christ. And concerning the return of Christ the Saviour plainly said, "Watch therefore, for ye know neither the day nor the hour wherein the Son of man cometh" (Matt. 25:13).

Again He said, "But of that day and hour knoweth no man, no, not the angels of heaven, but my Father only" (Matt. 24:36). Pentecost was one thing, but the restoration of the kingdom under Christ, Jesus told them, was an entirely different thing. Jesus is not now sitting on the throne of David, and the kingdom of Christ is not yet come.

Jesus Had Same Power Before Pentecost as After

"Church of Christ" people and some others usually believe that the reign of Christ on David's throne began at Pentecost. But the Scriptures do not say so. Actually, of course, Jesus on the day of Pentecost did not have any change of state or authority. Jesus had already risen from the dead with a glorified body fifty days before Pentecost. About ten days before Pentecost He had ascended to Heaven and sat down with the Father on His throne. Since His ascension, when He went up, up, till a cloud hid Him from the disciples' sight, the Scriptures do not hint that there has been any change whatever in the state of Jesus: His glory, power, authority or royalty. How could there be when He already had been glorified with the glory that He had with the Father in the beginning? (John 17:5).

In Matthew 28:18 we are told that Jesus said, before giving the Great Commission, *"All power is given unto me in heaven and in earth."* He did not say that all power or authority *will* be given, but He said "All power [or authority] *is given."* Jesus already, before His ascension, had received all authority in Heaven and in earth. He could not have more than that at Pentecost.

Nor are we to suppose that before His death and resurrection He lacked power and authority. He could have had twelve armies of angels for the asking at the time of His arrest (Matt. 26:53). He controlled demons with a word, at will, and repeatedly cast them out. He who in the beginning with the Father created the worlds used again the same creative power time after time during His earthly ministry. He created more loaves and fishes, He He put the coin in the fish's mouth, He gave life to the dead and changed the stinking, decaying body of Lazarus to breathing, pulsing health. Disease He cured with a word or thought. He was master of the wind, waves, angels, demons, life, death, Heaven and Hell, even in His earthly ministry, long before Pentecost.

Jesus in human form carried with Him all the power and authority of the Father. In His preaching He plainly said so, again and again. The Jews saw this and hated Him for it. John 5:18, 21–23 says:

> *"Therefore the Jews sought the more to kill him, because he not only had broken the sabbath, but said also that God was his Father, making himself equal with God."*
> *"For as the Father raiseth up the dead, and quickeneth them; even so the Son quickeneth whom he will. For the Father judgeth no man, but hath committed all judgment unto the Son: That all men should honour the Son, even as they honour the Father. He that honoureth not the Son honoureth not the Father which hath sent him."*

All judgment was committed to the Son; the Son had power to give life to "whom He will," and the Son must be honored as the Father. All this was true before Pentecost. Jesus at Pentecost did not get greater or less authority than He had before.

If on David's Throne Now, Why Not Before His Birth?

If Jesus is on David's throne now, then what is the difference in His reign now and that before He came to earth? He is one with the Father now, and has "the glory which I had with thee before the world was" (John 17:5). If He reigns *NOW* on David's throne, He reigned *THEN* on David's throne. There is only one throne ever mentioned in the Bible as being in Heaven, and that is the throne of God. Jesus sits there with the Father now on His throne (Rev. 3:21; Psa. 110:1). That throne was there before David ruled at Jerusalem; it is there now. It never has been, in the Bible, called the throne of David. David never sat on it. And Jesus, sitting on the throne with His Father until He receives His own kingdom and returns to reign, *IS NOT ON THE THRONE OF DAVID!* The reign of Christ on David's throne certainly did not begin at Pentecost.

World Hates Christ Now as in His Ministry

Is this world now subject to the reign of Christ as Israel was subject to David? The world does not love Him, the world does not obey Him. It crucified Him when He was here, and every Christ-rejecting sinner does the same thing in his heart. Peter denied Him, and the rest of the disciples forsook Him and fled. Do not present day disciples do the same?

What nation is a Christian nation in all the world today, as Israel was David's nation? Is America, with legalized booze, with the national government a party to the booze trade? Is the will of Christ done on earth as it is in Heaven, as Jesus taught it would be when the prayer, "Thy kingdom come," is answered? Look about you and see if the kingdoms of this world have been taken from Satan, "the god of this world" (II Cor. 4:4), and have been given to 'the Lord and His Christ.' No, not yet, but they will be at His coming.

Restoration of the Kingdom Not Till Jesus Comes, Says Peter

Preaching again in Acts 3:19–21, Peter urged the Jewish rulers and the Jewish nation to repent so that the national sins of Israel should be forgiven. But Peter plainly told them that those national sins for which Israel was suffering then and has suffered ever since would not be blotted out until the times of refreshing from the Lord, in the future, when at the second coming of Christ all the things promised by the prophets would be restored. Read carefully that passage.

> *"Repent ye therefore, and be converted, that your sins may be blotted out, when the times of refreshing shall come from the presence of the Lord; And he shall send Jesus Christ, which before was preached unto you: Whom the heaven must receive until the times of restitution of all things, which God hath spoken by the mouth of all his holy prophets since the world began."*
> —Acts 3:19–21.

The restitution of the kingdom of David and of other things promised by the prophets will not take place, this passage states, until Jesus comes again. The restitution of the nation Israel to the land of Canaan, and all the eternal and unchangeable promises of God to Israel, to Abraham's seed and to David's throne, await the second coming of Christ! Jesus is not now on David's throne.

"Times of refreshing shall come from the presence of the Lord," says Acts 3:19. That time of refreshing is also called "times of restitution" (verse 21). This time of refreshing or restitution will occur when the Father "shall send Jesus Christ" "whom the heaven must receive until the times of restitution." At that blessed time of the restitution of all things, the sins of national Israel shall be blotted out, and they shall be restored as a nation to favor with God.

The sins of individuals are blotted out when they repent. But to these Jewish leaders of the nation who officially rejected and crucified the Saviour, Peter preaches that they are to repent, that the sins mentioned, of Israel as a nation, would be blotted out at the second coming of Christ. Individual Jews do repent and their sins are blotted out as individuals. Then they are no longer condemned (John 3:18; John 5:24). But Israel as a whole will be forgiven and restored nationally, their kingdom will be restored, their land will be restored, at the second coming of Christ, and not till then.

This return of Christ is indicated more than once when the Lord discussed the restoration of Israel. Deuteronomy 30:3, speaking about the regathering of Israel and their restoration to their land, says, "That then the Lord thy God will turn thy captivity, and have compassion upon thee, and will return and gather thee from all the nations, whither the Lord thy God hath scattered thee." The term "Lord" in the Old Testament Scriptures often refers to Christ and seems to do so here. "The Lord . . . will return and gather thee from all the nations," said God to Israel. The regathering and restoration of Israel awaits the Lord's return!

Christ Gone to Receive a Kingdom—Will Return to Rule

The parable of the pounds given by the Saviour in Luke 19:12–27 clearly pictures the fact that the reign of Christ awaits His return from Heaven. This parable was given to explain why the kingdom did not immediately appear. The preceding verse, Luke 19:11, says: "And as they heard these things, he added and spake a parable, because he was nigh to Jerusalem, and because they thought that the kingdom of God should immediately appear." To correct this erroneous impression "that the kingdom of God should immediately appear," Jesus told them the parable of the pounds. This parable teaches that Jesus, in His ministry on earth, was like a nobleman with no kingdom; that He went away to

Heaven, and that when the Father gives Him the kingdom He will return, will reward faithful servants and destroy those who are not willing for Him to reign over them. Read the story for yourself.

"And as they heard these things, he added and spake a parable, because he was nigh to Jerusalem, and because they thought that the kingdom of God should immediately appear. He said therefore, A certain nobleman went into a far country to receive for himself a kingdom, and to return. And he called his ten servants, and delivered them ten pounds, and said unto them, Occupy till I come. But his citizens hated him, and sent a message after him, saying, We will not have this man to reign over us. And it came to pass, that when he was returned, having received the kingdom, then he commanded these servants to be called unto him, to whom he had given the money, that he might know how much every man had gained by trading. Then came the first, saying, Lord, thy pound hath gained ten pounds. And he said unto him, Well, thou good servant: because thou hast been faithful in a very little, have thou authority over ten cities. And the second came, saying, Lord, thy pound hath gained five pounds. And he said likewise to him, Be thou also over five cities."

For brevity's sake we leave out the verses about the unfaithful servant, and give you the last verse of the parable.

"But those mine enemies, which would not that I should reign over them, bring hither, and slay them before me."

Some great facts stand out in this parable.

1. In His first coming, Jesus was like a nobleman, deserving a kingdom, but having not yet entered into His rule. At the first coming of Christ, He did not sit on David's throne.

2. Jesus ascended to Heaven to "receive for himself a kingdom and to return." Jews there would understand that. It was as if Herod, a nobleman, should go to Rome and there persuade Caesar, the emperor of the whole Roman world, to appoint him as king in Judea. Having received the kingdom from the emperor, Herod would return to Jerusalem to reign.

3. In His absence, while Jesus is gone to the far country, we His servants are to "Occupy till I come." During this church or

gospel age, while we are carrying on the work of Christ, we are merely occupying until He receives the kingdom and returns to reign.

4. The reign does not begin until Christ, having received the kingdom, returns. After His return, the nobleman, having received the kingdom, says to one servant, "Have thou authority over ten cities," to another He says, "Be thou also over five cities." A king appoints his helpers to rule with him at the beginning of his kingdom. A president appoints his cabinet when he goes into office. So Christ, when He returns, will appoint faithful Christians to rule with Him, each one according to his faithfulness and ability.

Likewise, at the beginning of his reign, a man must put down his enemies. A peaceful reign is impossible until rebels are put down. So in Luke 19:27, Jesus teaches us that when He returns and reigns from the throne of His glory, David's throne, and faithful servants rule over literal cities with Him on this earth, that living enemies who do not consent to His rule will be put to death. How clearly this pictures the battle of Armageddon and the judgment of the living Gentiles as pictured in Matthew 25:31–46.

Surely the parable of the pounds proves that Jesus is gone into a far country and that when the Father gives Him the kingdom He will return to rule on this earth in the promised kingdom, will appoint faithful ones to rule with Him and destroy His enemies.

The same connection between the second coming of Christ and His reign is found in Revelation 2:25–27, where Christians are commanded to "hold fast till I come" and then are promised that those overcoming will rule over the nations, even as God has promised to Jesus.

"But that which ye have already hold fast till I come. And he that overcometh, and keepeth my works unto the end, to him will I give power over the nations: And he shall rule them with a rod of iron; as the vessels of a potter shall they be broken to shivers: even as I received of my Father."—Rev. 2:25–27.

The connection and order of events here is very clear. Christians are now to hold fast and live the overcoming life "till I come." Then when Jesus comes He will reward overcoming Christians with the right to rule with Him "over the nations."

Verse 27 quotes Psalm 2:9. That Psalm tells about the reign of Christ on earth. Revelation 2:26 says that Christians will reign with Him. And in connection with Revelation 2:25, it plainly says that this will be at the second coming of Christ. Christians who hold fast until Jesus comes, that is, overcoming Christians, will rule with Christ when He sits as King "upon my holy hill of Zion" (Psalm 2:6).

The Tabernacle of David, Now Fallen Down, to Be Rebuilt When Christ Returns

A great commotion took place among the Hebrew Christians when Paul began his missionary tours among the Gentiles. A great discussion arose as to whether Gentiles could be saved by faith in Christ without being circumcised and keeping the law of Moses. Paul, Barnabas and others went up to Jerusalem to meet the apostles and there threshed the thing out. All came to the conclusion that it was the will of God for Gentiles to be saved, that God should take out of the Gentiles a people for His name, and He would afterwards return and build again the tabernacle of David which was fallen down. The tabernacle of David, his kingly reign and throne, has fallen down. But when Jesus returns it will be restored. Read Acts 15:13–16 and you will see that clearly the reign of Christ is to come when HE RETURNS to the earth.

"And after they had held their peace, James answered, saying, Men and brethren, hearken unto me: Simeon hath declared how God at the first did visit the Gentiles, to take out of them a people for his name. And to this agree the words of the prophets; as it is written, After this I will RETURN, and will build again the tabernacle of David, which is fallen down; and I will build again the ruins thereof, and I will set it up."

God is now taking out a people for His name among the Gentiles, but the Lord Jesus will return and build again the tabernacle of David. Isaiah 16:5 shows clearly that the tabernacle of David means a throne where Christ will rule.

A similar thought is found in the eleventh chapter of Romans where the Holy Spirit tells us that "blindness in part is happened to Israel, until the fulness of the Gentiles be come in" (Romans 11:25), but after that Israel shall be saved. Jews are now blinded and about the hardest of all people to reach with the gospel. But when Jesus returns, those left alive will be saved, when the tabernacle of David is built again and Christ reigns.

That time will be "the regeneration" when the apostles will reign with Him, sitting on twelve thrones and judging the twelve tribes of Israel (Matt. 19:28).

Christ Now Seated With the Father in His Throne, Not on the Throne of David

In Revelation 3:21 we are plainly told where Jesus now is. He sits, not on the throne of David, but on the right hand of His Father, in the Father's throne. "To him that overcometh will I grant to sit with me in my throne, even as I also overcame, and am set down with my Father in his throne" (Rev. 3:21). In the future, this passage teaches, Jesus will sit on His own throne. Then Jesus will allow others who overcome to reign with Him, just as the Father allows Jesus to sit with Him in His throne.

God the Father has an agreement with His Son Jesus Christ about this matter, which is mentioned in the 110th Psalm. There we are told that the Father has invited the Son to sit on His right hand until all His enemies are made the footstool of Jesus, and that then He shall reign out of Zion, that is, out of the city of Jerusalem. We give here the entire 110th Psalm.

"The Lord said unto my Lord, Sit thou at my right hand, until I make thine enemies thy footstool. 2 The Lord shall send the rod of thy strength out of Zion: rule thou in the midst of thine enemies. 3 Thy people shall be willing in the day of thy power, in the beauties of holiness from the womb of the morning: thou hast the dew of thy youth. 4 The Lord hath sworn, and will not repent, Thou art a priest for ever after the order of Melchizedek. 5 The Lord at thy right hand shall strike through kings in the day of his wrath. 6 He shall judge among the heathen, he shall fill the places with the dead bodies; he shall wound the heads over many countries. 7 He shall drink of the brook in the way: therefore shall he lift up the head."

Jesus, then, is not now sitting on the throne of David but is seated at the right hand of the Father in His throne. When the time comes for the reign of Christ, then the terrible retribution, mentioned in this Psalm, verses 2, 5, and 6, will take place on the enemies of Christ. Later we shall learn that these refer to the Great Tribulation and battle of Armageddon when "he shall smite the earth with the rod of his mouth, and with the breath of his lips shall he slay the wicked" (Isa. 11:4; II Thess. 2:8).

But Christ is not now on David's throne. David, on a throne at Jerusalem, and Christ in Heaven, have nothing in common as kings. David was on earth, Christ is not. David ruled over a nation of Jews, Christ does not rule over a nation of Jews. The Jews, by a great majority, rejected Christ as both King and Saviour. They said, "We will not have this man to reign over us" (Luke 19:14). Even today the vast majority of Jews will have nothing to do with Christ. The land of Palestine is inhabited largely by Mohammedans who do not even acknowledge the deity of Christ, much less accept Him as Saviour and King.

The Un-kingly Jesus

This Nazarene peasant, do you call Him a king? David was rich beyond imagination, a monarch whose glory shames the crowned heads of Europe. But Jesus had nowhere to lay His head. He had no money to pay taxes until God put a coin in the mouth of a fish. He had no bed in which to be born, no grave in which to be laid, but in birth and in death was the object of charity. He ate His daily bread as a penniless one supported by the ministrations of good women. His estate, after the nails were driven in His hands, and His naked body had died on the cross, was one simple garment, a seamless robe! No, Christ had all the powers of a king, but He did not exercise them in His brief ministry on this earth. He who thought it not robbery to be equal with God had voluntarily emptied Himself, and became, not a King, but a Saviour; not rich, but poor; not proud, but meek and lowly in heart.

A king? No, the wise men who brought Him gifts, as to a king, looked far into the distant future when Christ should reign over the Jews. A king? To be sure it was written of Him by Pilate, but it was written above the cross where He was crucified! I think that even Pilate, Pilate the compromiser, Pilate the cowardly one, Pilate the pleaser of men, the seeker after human favor—even Pilate seemed to know that Christ would come into His own and would one day reign as a king.

A king? No, the only crown He wore was a crown of thorns, briars pressed down on His dear head in mockery. The only scepter He ever wielded, the only kingly robe He ever wore, was after He was scourged with the Roman cat-o'-nine-tails, when the mocking soldiers plucked out His beard, blindfolded Him and beat Him over the head and people said, "Guess who hit you." That bleeding, stumbling figure, carrying the cross out of the gate of Jerusalem to the place of a skull—do you call Him a king? Is there any likeness between this abused, despised, and pitiful figure, the jest of the soldiers, the pawn of Herod and Pilate, the One despised and rejected by Israel; is there any likeness, I say, between Him and King David the mighty monarch of Jerusalem with his great palace, his riches, his power and the applause of the world? No! By faith we know the kingly heart of the Saviour, but we must admit that Christ did not rule as a king. At His first coming Jesus did not rule as King of the Jews. He did not then, and He does not now, sit on David's throne. The kingdom of Christ on earth has not yet begun.

When Will Jesus Sit on His Throne, the Throne of David?

So much is said about the coming reign of Christ in the Bible that we should expect definite teaching about when Christ will sit on His throne and reign. Thank God, we do have definite teaching in many places on this question. For instance Matthew 25:31. There the Saviour tells us, "When the Son of man shall come in his glory, and all the holy angels with him, then shall he sit upon the throne of his glory." When will Jesus sit on His throne, His promised throne, to reign over His promised kingdom? The Scripture answers, "When the Son of man shall come in his glory . . . THEN shall he sit upon the throne of his glory." All the argument in the world cannot change the plain, simple fact which the Scripture expressly states: Jesus will be enthroned at His Second Coming.

Some may complain, however, that that Scripture, Matthew 25:31, refers to Jesus sitting on a throne to judge. It does tell about His judging those that are brought before Him, the sheep and goats, the saved and lost of the living nations on the earth when He returns. And that judgment will be on the basis of what they have done toward Christ's brethren, the Jews, during the tribulation period. We grant that. However, one must distinguish between this judgment of the living on earth with those three groups of sheep, goats and brethren, and the last great judgment of the unsaved dead, mentioned in Revelation 20:11-15. No, Matthew 25:31 tells of the beginning of His kingdom when He shall sit on the throne of His glory. Those brought before Him are the living of the nations of the earth over whom He is to rule. In fact, in the same context, Matthew 25:34, we are told that the Saviour will say to the saints who will reign with Him: "Come, ye blessed of my Father, inherit the kingdom prepared for you from the foundation of the world" (Matt. 25:34). The kingdom of Christ begins when He will sit on the throne of His glory at His coming.

In II Timothy 4:1, Paul plainly tells Timothy that the Lord Jesus Christ, "shall judge the quick and the dead at his appearing and his kingdom." "The quick," or living, will be judged at the appearing of Jesus to reign, and the dead will be judged before He turns the kingdom over to His Father. Get it clear in your mind that according to II Timothy 4:1 "his kingdom" comes after "his appearing."

Jesus is not sitting on His throne now, but He will sit on the throne of David at His Second Coming. Not in the rapture of the saints when we go up in the air to meet Him, but after our honeymoon in Heaven when Jesus comes visibly, bodily, literally, with all His holy angels to reign on this earth, "THEN shall He sit upon the throne of His glory." Certainly that kingdom is in the future, not the present. Do not be discouraged, dear Christian, for all God has promised He will do, and the Saviour shall have the kingdom that rightfully belongs to Him and shall reign on the throne of David on this earth.

Chapter 9

Eternal Promises to the City, Jerusalem

PREACHERS and Bible teachers have fallen into an evil way of spiritualizing the Word of God, explaining away the promises and making the Bible mean what it does not say. In many editions of the Bible, men have defiled the Word of God with their opinions which explain away the literal meaning of the inspired Book. At the top of pages or chapters where God promised good to Israel, men have written "God's promise to the church." When God's Word prophesies good to Jerusalem or to Mount Zion, or prophesies about the future of Mount Zion, such learned teachers and preachers often say that God did not mean what He said at all, but referred to Heaven. They are wrong, utterly, foolishly, presumptuously, wickedly wrong! The Bible says what it means and means what it says. God has an eternal plan connected with the literal city of Jerusalem in Palestine, which is so plainly foretold that honest Bible students must accept it. Mount Zion is "the southwest hill of Jerusalem, the older and higher part of the city; it is often called, the city of David" (Young's Analytical Concordance). The term "Mount Zion" is often used for the whole city of Jerusalem.

If you want to understand what God says in the Bible about Jerusalem, then remember this: always the name Jerusalem refers to the literal city of Jerusalem in Palestine, unless the Scripture indicates otherwise. Five times in the Bible, in Galatians 4:26, Hebrews 12:22, Revelation 3:12, Revelation 21:2, and Revelation 21:10, the word "Jerusalem" refers to the heavenly city which will one day come down to Palestine on the site of the old Jerusalem. Hundreds of times "Jerusalem" means the city now in Palestine.

The other five times it refers to the heavenly city which will one day be on the same site, literally and actually a new Jerusalem.

Likewise Mount Zion is used in the Bible scores of times as synonymous with the city of Jerusalem. Once, certainly (Heb. 12:22), possibly again (Rev. 14:1), Mount Zion is used as synonymous with the heavenly Jerusalem. The rest of the time, everywhere in the Bible, the term "Mount Zion" means the literal hill on which the older part of Jerusalem will be built, and it is used as synonymous with the city Jerusalem. If you would understand the Scriptures and know God's plans and promises, then take literally His promises about Jerusalem and Mount Zion.

Mount Moriah, Where Abraham Offered Isaac, the Site of the Temple and Jerusalem

God had selected Jerusalem as the permanent capital of Palestine and the center of temple worship, even before the children of Israel took the land. Did Abraham know, when he took his son Isaac three days journey to sacrifice him by faith on Mount Moriah, that Mount Moriah was the very spot where later Solomon would be instructed to build the temple? Perhaps by faith Abraham did know that, for we are told that he "looked for a city"! (Heb. 11:10). God had some purpose in bringing there to the temple site that sacrifice picturing the coming Saviour.

When the children of Israel were encamped west of the Jordan River, and Moses gave them their final instructions and charges before he should die and they should enter the promised land of Canaan, the Lord revealed to them that He would choose the place for His sacrifices and eventually for the temple, which He already had in mind. Deuteronomy 12:5, 6 says:

> *"But unto the place which the Lord your God shall choose out of all your tribes to put his name there, even unto his habitation shall ye seek, and thither thou shalt come: And thither ye shall bring your burnt offerings, and your sacrifices, and your tithes, and heave offerings of your hand, and your vows, and your free-will-offerings, and the firstlings of your herds and of your flocks."*

Five times in that chapter that place is mentioned, in only slightly different words, as 'the place which the Lord God shall choose to cause His name to dwell there.'

David was led to make his capital at Jerusalem when a great plague came on the entire nation because of David's sin in numbering the people.

> *"And when the angel stretched out his hand upon Jerusalem to destroy it, the Lord repented him of the evil, and said to the angel that destroyed the people, It is enough: stay now thine hand. And the angel of the Lord was by the threshingplace of Araunah the Jebusite. And David spake unto the Lord when he saw the angel that smote the people, and said, Lo, I have sinned, and I have done wickedly: but these sheep, what have they done? let thine hand, I pray thee, be against me, and against my father's house. And Gad came that day to David, and said unto him, Go up, rear an altar unto the Lord in the threshingfloor of Araunah the Jebusite."*—II Sam. 24:16–18.

In obedience to the Lord's command by the mouth of the prophet Gad, David bought the threshingfloor of Araunah and built there "an altar to the Lord" and the plague was stayed.

GOD HAD HIS HEART SET ON JERUSALEM! Looking down through the years to His future plans for the city, God loved it and would not let it be destroyed. He said to the angel, "Stay now thine hand"!

The Threshingfloor of Araunah Was the Site of Solomon's Temple

And what about this threshingfloor of Araunah, or Ornan? It was on the very spot where God would later have His temple built by Solomon, David's Son!

II Chronicles 3:1 tells us, "Then Solomon began to build the house of the Lord at Jerusalem in mount Moriah, where the Lord appeared unto David his father, in the place that David had prepared in the threshingfloor of Ornan the Jebusite." Where God commanded Abraham to offer his son Isaac as a sacrifice is where God commanded David to offer a sacrifice to stay the plague. There God His temple built, the place of sacrifice.

From the beginning God planned an eternal destiny for Jerusalem and its holy environs.

God's Name Placed Perpetually at Jerusalem

God placed His name at Jerusalem forever, and His plan for the city and the temple site reaches on into the literal reign of Christ on earth when all Israel shall be regathered to their own land, and when that great Seed of David shall return and establish forever David's throne and rule thereon. In I Kings 9:1-3 we are told how God has made an unchanging choice of the site of the temple and of Jerusalem.

"And it came to pass, when Solomon had finished the building of the house of the Lord, and the king's house, and all Solomon's desire which he was pleased to do, That the Lord appeared to Solomon the second time, as he had appeared unto him at Gibeon. And the Lord said unto him, I have heard thy prayer and thy supplication, that thou hast made before me: I have hallowed this house, which thou hast built, TO PUT MY NAME THERE FOR EVER; AND MINE EYES AND MINE HEART SHALL BE THERE PERPETUALLY."—I Kings 9:1-3.

The same thing is told in II Chronicles 7:15, 16 in the following words:

"Now mine eyes shall be open, and mine ears attent unto the prayer that is made in this place. For now have I chosen and sanctified this house, that my name may be there for ever: and mine eyes and mine heart shall be there perpetually."

Note that God said that He would place there His name, His eyes, His heart! God's name, on this earth, He wants ever connected with the city Jerusalem! His eyes watch continually over that place! His heart is there! Notice, too, that God said this was "for ever," and again "perpetually." Even about Jerusalem, then, the Scripture is true that "the gifts and calling of God are without repentance" (Rom. 11:29). God will not change His plans concerning that city Jerusalem and the site of His temple there on Mount Moriah. It must have been for this reason that God repented of the evil that He had planned to do to Jerusalem and said to the angel He had sent to destroy it, "Stay now thine hand" (I Chron. 21:15; II Sam. 24:16).

All the prophets of the Old Testament knew about God's

eternal purpose and covenant concerning Jerusalem, and it is often mentioned. Notice the following Scriptures:

"For David said, The Lord God of Israel hath given rest unto his people, that they may dwell in Jerusalem for ever."
—I Chron. 23:25.

"Also he built altars in the house of the Lord, whereof the Lord had said, In Jerusalem shall my name be for ever."
—II Chron. 33:4.

"And he set a graven image of the grove that he had made in the house, of which the Lord said to David, and to Solomon his son, In this house, and in Jerusalem, which I have chosen out of all tribes of Israel, will I put my name for ever."—II Kings 21:7.

Joel tells us of the time when Christ shall be "the Lord your God dwelling in Zion, my holy mountain: then shall Jerusalem be holy, and there shall no strangers pass through her any more" (Joel 3:17). In that time, we are told: "But Judah shall dwell for ever, and Jerusalem from generation to generation. For I will cleanse their blood that I have not cleansed: for the Lord dwelleth in Zion" (Joel 3:20–21). Surely Joel, writing the prophecy, knew God's plan to place His name perpetually at Jerusalem as the center and joy of the whole earth, the city of the Great King.

Micah foretold that Jerusalem was to be the center of the plan of Christ on earth. Notice the terms: "the mountain of the house of the Lord," "the mountain of the Lord," "the house of the God of Jacob," "Zion," "Jerusalem." These words mean just what they say. The "house" is the temple at Jerusalem. The "mountain" is the literal Mount Zion on which the older part of Jerusalem was built. Mount Moriah is the site of the temple adjoining Mount Zion, and is within the city. In the Bible the prophets everywhere used such terms referring to the city of Jerusalem. Micah said:

"But in the last days it shall come to pass, that the mountain of the house of the Lord shall be established in the top of the mountains, and it shall be exalted above the hills; and people shall flow unto it. And many nations shall come, and say, Come, and let us go up to the mountain of the Lord, and to the house of the God of Jacob; and he will teach us of his ways, and we will walk

in his paths: for the law shall go forth of Zion, and the word of the Lord from Jerusalem."—Micah 4:1, 2.

"And I will make her that halted a remnant, and her that was cast far off a strong nation: and the Lord shall reign over them in mount Zion from henceforth, even for ever."—Micah 4:7.

Isaiah tells us that:

"In that day shall the branch of the Lord be beautiful and glorious, and the fruit of the earth shall be excellent and comely for them that are escaped of Israel. And it shall come to pass, that he that is left in Zion, and he that remaineth in Jerusalem, shall be called holy, even every one that is written among the living in Jerusalem."—Isa. 4:2, 3.

This glory to be on Jerusalem is yet future, as verses 5 and 6 of the same chapter undeniably show.

Daniel and Nehemiah Knew God's Eternal Plan for Jerusalem

The prophets seem to have known how God always looked upon Jerusalem. For this reason, Daniel, captive in the foreign land of Babylon, prayed three times a day with his window open toward Jerusalem (Dan. 6:10). For this reason Daniel prayed,

"O Lord, according to all thy righteousness, I beseech thee, let thine anger and thy fury be turned away from THY CITY JE-RUSALEM, THY HOLY MOUNTAIN: because for our sins, and for the iniquities of our fathers, JERUSALEM and thy people are become a reproach to all that are about us. Now therefore, O our God, hear the prayer of thy servant, and his supplications, and cause thy face to shine upon THY SANCTUARY THAT IS DESOLATE, for the Lord's sake. O my God, incline thine ear, and hear; open thine eyes, and behold our desolations, and the city which is called by thy name: for we do not present our supplications before thee for our righteousnesses, but for thy great mercies. O Lord, hear; O Lord, forgive; O Lord, hearken and do; defer not, for thine own sake, O my God: FOR THY CITY AND THY PEOPLE ARE CALLED BY THY NAME."

—Dan. 9:16–19.

Daniel knew that though the city of Jerusalem then lay waste, that God Himself would see that it was rebuilt. Though the temple, the sanctuary of God, was then vacant, God Himself had placed His name there perpetually! Daniel knew that God had further plans for Palestine and Israel and the city Jerusalem and the site of the temple there!

Nehemiah, knowing God's promises about the city, fasted and prayed with weeping when he heard that the wall of Jerusalem was broken down and the gates thereof were burned with fire. Something of this must have been in the heart of Jesus Himself when He looked on the city He loved and said:

"O Jerusalem, Jerusalem, thou that killest the prophets, and stonest them which are sent unto thee, how often would I have gathered thy children together, even as a hen gathereth her chickens under her wings, and ye would not! Behold, your house is left unto you desolate. For I say unto you, Ye shall not see me henceforth, till ye shall say, Blessed is he that cometh in the name of the Lord."—Matt. 23:37–39.

In these brief verses, how much is told! The love of Jesus for the Holy City, Jerusalem, and for the Jews; the certain destruction of the city and the temple; and also, thank God, we are told that Israel, in Jerusalem, shall one day cry out, when they see Jesus in person, "Blessed is He that cometh in the name of the Lord!"

Jerusalem, "the City of the Great King"

In the prophets and Psalms, Jerusalem is a famous theme. In Psalm 48:1, 2, the importance of Jerusalem in the plan of God is shown.

"Great is the Lord, and greatly to be praised in the city of our God, in the mountain of his holiness. Beautiful for situation, the joy of the whole earth, is mount Zion, on the sides of the north, the city of the great King."

The Psalmist wrote, not primarily for his own time, but looking into the future, he was inspired to know that the time would come when Jerusalem should be "the joy of the whole earth." Jerusalem was "the city of the great King," but that King mentioned was not David nor Solomon, but a coming King. Jesus Himself quoted that phrase in Matthew 5:35 saying that none should swear by Jerusalem "for it is the city of the great King." There would be no blasphemy in taking the name of a man in vain. This great King is Jesus, the Son of God, very God Himself. No one should swear by Jerusalem, because it is the city of Jesus, the great King—not because it is the city of King David. This proves surely that the literal city of Jerusalem will be the center of the reign of Christ.

That coming great King will sit on His throne at Jerusalem, and then Jerusalem shall be the joy of the whole earth. When the Saviour returns to reign, when Israel is regathered and converted, when Jesus sits in the literal city of Jerusalem on the throne of David, then these prophecies about Jerusalem will be fulfilled.

Jerusalem Will Be "the Joy of the Whole Earth"

In the days of David and Solomon, Jerusalem was a great city. The wealth of Jerusalem was its temple, palaces, and princes which were widely known. But Jerusalem was not "the joy of the whole earth." Other cities had their palaces and kings reigning over more people than David or Solomon. Other cities had their worship of idols and heathen deities, attended by more people than the worship of God at Jerusalem. David was a king, but not THE great King. These verses were not then fulfilled:

"Great is the Lord, and greatly to be praised in the city of our God, in the mountain of his holiness. Beautiful for situation, the joy of the whole earth, is mount Zion, on the sides of the north, the city of the great King."—Psa. 48:1-2.

Nor were they fulfilled in the personal ministry of Christ. Rome, not Jerusalem, was the center of the world. The people of the whole earth did not take joy in Jerusalem. Jerusalem was "the city of the Great King" only in prospect, for they crucified their King, and He did not reign in Jerusalem.

Jerusalem is not now "the joy of the whole earth." The holy mountain is traversed alike by pagan, Mohammedan, infidel, Jew and stranger. Nor does the great King reign there. No, this blessed prophecy that "Beautiful for situation, the joy of the whole earth, is mount Zion, on the sides of the north, the city of the great King," simply means that God has eternal purposes for Jerusalem. It will be "the city of the great King," "the joy of the whole earth," when Christ rules from the throne of David over the whole earth.

The Pillar of Cloud and Fire Which Led Israel in the Wilderness, Will Be Over Jerusalem in the Kingdom Age

When Christ returns, when Israel is gathered, judged, and then, as the Holy Spirit tells us through the prophet Isaiah, the pillar of cloud by day and the fire by night which led Israel in the wilderness, will abide over the city Jerusalem. Read now the last of that fourth chapter of Isaiah.

"When the Lord shall have washed away the filth of the daughters of Zion, and shall have purged the blood of JERUSALEM from the midst thereof by the spirit of judgment, and by the spirit of burning. And the Lord will create upon every dwelling place of MOUNT ZION, and upon her assemblies, a cloud and smoke by day, and the shining of a flaming fire by night: for upon all the glory shall be a defence. And there shall be a tabernacle for a shadow in the daytime from the heat, and for a place of refuge, and for a covert from storm and from rain."

This prophecy is to be fulfilled in Jerusalem. It could not be the heavenly Jerusalem, because it will come when "the Lord shall have washed away the filth of the daughters of Zion, and shall have purged the blood of Jerusalem from the midst thereof by the spirit of judgment, and by the spirit of burning." The heavenly Jerusalem has never needed purging, and the Heavenly Jerusalem has never had the blood of violence.

Israel is to be regathered from all the earth, and in the wilderness of wanderings they will be assembled where the Saviour will plead with them face to face (Ezek. 20:33–44). At that time the rebels will be purged out and the remnant will "pass under the rod" and God will bring them "into the bond of the covenant." When that judgment shall have taken place, when the Lord shall have washed away the filth of the daughters of Zion and purged the blood of Jerusalem, then we are told that the eternal presence of God over the city will be pictured day and night by the pillar of cloud and of fire.

When the Lord brought the children of Israel out of Egypt, we are told that

"The Lord went before them by day in a pillar of a cloud, to lead them the way; and by night in a pillar of fire, to give them light; to go by day and night: He took not away the pillar of the cloud by day, nor the pillar of fire by night, from before the people."—Exod. 13:21, 22.

The Lord was in the pillar of cloud and of fire. With that pillar of cloud He led them in the daytime; in the fire He watched over them by night. From that cloud and fire He defended them against the Egyptians (Exod. 14:24, 25). It was the visible evidence of His presence with His people. That cloudy pillar descended, after Israel's sin in the matter of the golden calf, and from that pillar, the Lord talked with Moses (Exod. 33:9, 10). Over the tabernacle, day and night, was this cloud of the Lord in the sight of all Israel and through all their journeys (Exod. 40:38). God was leading His people from their bondage in Egypt into their own land.

But again the children of Israel are in bondage. They are scattered throughout all the world. They have no temple, no priesthood, no sacrifices. They have rejected their Messiah and crucified their King. The wrath of God is upon them. But one day He will gather them again to the "wilderness of wanderings," purge out the rebels, cleanse the city Jerusalem, and entering that lovely city, will make that His home, His throne, His temple! At that day, the cloud of the Lord will cover every dwelling place in the city of Jerusalem; and at night, as a flaming fire, He will be visible above all the city where He has sworn that forever His name, His eyes, and His heart shall be. Then Jerusalem shall be the city of the great King.

The River That Shall Flow From Jerusalem in the Kingdom Age

How many details God gives us about the marvelous kingdom age that is coming! It is sad that multitudes of Bible students have ignored or explained away the wonderful promises of God's Word concerning the coming kingdom. But it is a happy truth that enough is revealed for the careful, prayerful, humble student of God's Word to have a clear picture in mind concerning this future kingdom. Many physical details concerning that kingdom, the nation, the throne, and the city Jerusalem cannot be imagined as having taken place. For instance, the pillar of fire and cloud prophesied in Isaiah 4:5 has never stood over every dwelling place in Jerusalem.

So it is with the wonderful river of water which shall flow forth from Jerusalem during the kingdom age.

At present there is no river at Jerusalem and there has never been. The nearest river is the Jordan, several miles away. The tiny brook Kidron (Cedron) which flows on the east of Jerusalem, has never been called a river, and it is not in the city of Jerusalem. But the Scriptures tell us that the time will come when a great river will flow out from the city of Jerusalem, originating where the temple did stand.

The Garden of Eden had a river which "went out of Eden to water the garden" (Gen. 2:10). The new Jerusalem, the heavenly city, will have also a river, "a pure river of water of life, clear as crystal, proceeding out of the throne of God and of the Lamb" (Rev. 22:1). Now study with me a bit and learn the interesting fact that these two, the Garden of Eden and Heaven, will both be united in the literal city Jerusalem, in Palestine, and that the river of water of life will flow out from the site of the ancient temple there.

The Psalmist tells us: "There is a river, the streams whereof shall make glad the city of God, the holy place of the tabernacles of the most High" (Psa. 46:4). The time mentioned is future. In your Bible you will find the words "there is" in italics, meaning those words were not in the original. The time is not present, but future. "The streams whereof SHALL make glad the city of God."

The rest of the Psalm makes clear the time spoken of is future. Verse 5 of the same Psalm says: "God is in the midst of her; she shall not be moved: God shall help her, and that right early." The river will make glad the city when God is in the midst of her. Verse 6 next tells about the moving of the kingdoms and the melting of the earth when God shall speak. Verse 8 tells of the terrible tribulation He will bring before His kingdom. Verse 9 then tells us that "He maketh wars to cease unto the end of the earth; he breaketh the bow, and cutteth the spear in sunder; he burneth the chariot in the fire" (Psa. 46:9). When God makes wars to cease, then the Kingdom of Christ will be begun, and then verse 10 tells us that God "will be exalted in the earth." So during the kingdom age, we are told about "a river, the streams whereof shall make glad the city of God, the holy place of the tabernacles of the most High."

That River Begins to Flow at The Second Coming of Christ

The river mentioned is a literal river of water, and the city of God is the literal city of Jerusalem. How do we know? Because the Scripture expressly tells us how that river will spring up at Jerusalem, at the second coming of Christ.

Zechariah 14 is a clear picture of the return of Christ and of the battle of Armageddon. Compare it with Revelation 19:11–21 and you can see that it is the same. The Lord will return from Heaven to reign on the earth. He will bring with Him His saints (Zech. 14:5) who will have been resurrected and translated before this and caught out to meet Him in the air. He will find Jerusalem compassed with the armies of the Antichrist and the city itself falling under the onslaught of the armies of the world, under the leadership of the wicked Man of Sin (Zech. 14:1, 2). The Lord will fight against these nations and utterly destroy them in that day (Zech. 14:3, Rev. 19:20, 21).

The Lord shall stand with His feet upon the Mount of Olives in that day (Zech. 14:4), and violent physical changes shall take place, "and the mount of Olives shall cleave in the midst thereof toward the east and toward the west, and there shall be a very great valley." It will probably be caused by an earthquake, and the people shall flee from it as they have from other earthquakes (vs. 5). And then in the same chapter we are told about the river that shall spring up in Jerusalem, in that day, when the Lord shall be King over all the earth.

"And it shall be in that day, that living waters shall go out from Jerusalem; half of them toward the former sea, and half of them toward the hinder sea: in summer and in winter shall it be. And the Lord shall be king over all the earth: in that day shall there be one Lord, and his name one."—Zech. 14:8, 9.

The river mentioned is a literal river, just as the Mount of Olives mentioned in the same chapter is a literal mountain. The literal city Jerusalem shall be attacked by the armies of all nations and rescued by the Lord from Heaven. And IN THE SAME DAY the living waters shall flow out from the literal city of Jerusalem. This is the "river, the streams whereof shall make glad the city of God."

The River Will Spring Out From Under the Temple at Jerusalem

Several chapters in the book of Ezekiel are given over by the Holy Spirit to a detailed discussion of the temple, the sacrifices, the worship and other physical details concerning Jerusalem and the land during the reign of Christ. Chapters 34 to 37 repeat again and again the promise of the restoration of the people of Israel to their land as a nation. Chapters 40 to 46 tell about the temple at Jerusalem, the place of God's throne there, the altar and worship. Then Ezekiel 47:1, 2 tell the details about that wonderful river, "the streams whereof shall make glad the city of God," mentioned by the Psalmist. We are told:

"Afterward he brought me again unto the door of the house; and, behold, waters issued out from under the threshold of the house eastward: for the forefront of the house stood toward the east, and the waters came down from under from the right side of the house, at the south side of the altar. Then brought he me out of the way of the gate northward, and led me about the way without unto the utter gate by the way that looketh eastward; and, behold, there ran out waters on the right side."

Ezekiel tells how the angel measured the water and found it first ankle deep, then to the knee, then to the loins, and then water deep enough to swim in, too deep to wade.

Other verses of the passage continue the story of how this wonderful river will flow out from Jerusalem and go to the sea. Zechariah 14:8 tells us that the waters will divide "half of them toward the former sea, and half of them toward the hinder sea," that is, half to the Mediterranean Sea, and half toward the Dead Sea. Ezekiel tells us how the waters from this river that make glad

the city of God will heal the Dead Sea until it will not any more be the salt sea as it is now. Verses 8 to 11 say:

> "*Then said he unto me, These waters issue out toward the east country, and go down into the desert, and go into the sea: which being brought forth into the sea, the waters shall be healed. And it shall come to pass, that every thing that liveth, which moveth, whithersoever the rivers shall come, shall live: and there shall be a very great multitude of fish, because these waters shall come thither: for they shall be healed; and every thing shall live whither the river cometh. And it shall come to pass, that the fishers shall stand upon it from En-gedi even unto En-eglaim; they shall be a place to spread forth nets; their fish shall be according to their kinds, as the fish of the great sea, exceeding many. But the miry places thereof and the marishes thereof shall not be healed; they shall be given to salt.*"—Ezek. 47:8–11.

Note that this is not somewhere up in the heavens, but on earth. This river will flow out from Jerusalem, and half of it will go eastward into the Dead Sea. There fish will live and fishers will fish and spread their nets. Salt marshes will be left, because in the kingdom age we will eat the fish and salt them with salt even as Jesus ate a piece of a broiled fish and an honeycomb (Luke 24:42, 43) after His resurrection.

This is the river of water of life. In the same chapter, Ezekiel 47, verses 7 and 12 say:

> "*Now when I had returned, behold, at the bank of the river were very many trees on the one side and on the other.*"
> —Verse 7.
> "*And by the river upon the bank thereof, on this side and on that side, shall grow all trees for meat, whose leaf shall not fade, neither shall the fruit thereof be consumed: it shall bring forth new fruit according to his months, because their waters they issued out of the sanctuary: and the fruit thereof shall be for meat, and the leaf thereof for medicine.*"—Verse 12.

The river is the river of life. The trees are the trees of life, for the same story is told in Revelation 22:1, 2. Compare Ezekiel 47:7, 12, with Revelation 22:1, 2.

"And he shewed me a pure river of water of life, clear as crystal, proceeding out of the throne of God and of the Lamb. In the midst of the street of it, and on either side of the river, was there the tree of life, which bare twelve manner of fruits, and yielded her fruit every month: and the leaves of the tree were for the healing of the nations."—Rev. 22:1, 2.

This passage in Revelation certainly is telling about the heavenly Jerusalem which will come down to earth from God the Father and will abide on the site of the old Jerusalem as the capital city of the world. The book of Revelation makes clear that this heavenly Jerusalem will come down at the close of the thousand years' reign of Christ when the Father comes down to take over the reins of government with His Son (I Cor. 15:24; Rev. 21:2, 3), but during the thousand years and afterwards, the promises are to Jerusalem, just the same. The river will flow from Jerusalem, making glad the city of God. And this river of water of life will have beside it on either bank, the trees of life which bear twelve manner of fruits and whose leaves are for the healing of the nations.

Honest hearts will rejoice in the promises of God, and will long to see that lovely city Jerusalem when it becomes actually "the joy of the whole earth . . . the city of the great King," with the river of God to make it glad! (Psa. 48:2).

The prophecy of Zechariah has much to say about that coming time when, during the Great Tribulation, Jerusalem will be oppressed under the Antichrist. The name Jerusalem appears in those brief fourteen chapters thirty-nine times! Read the following verses: "In that day there shall be a fountain opened to the house of David and to the inhabitants of Jerusalem for sin and for uncleanness" (Zech. 13:1).

Zechariah tells of the trouble in Jerusalem at that time, but he also tells of how salvation will come to Jerusalem, when her King comes. The fourteenth chapter tells how the Antichrist will bring his armies against the literal city of Jerusalem to sack and destroy it, but the same chapter tells how Jesus will return in person to save that literal city Jerusalem. Then "his feet shall stand in that day upon the mount of Olives which is before Jerusalem on the east" (Zech. 14:4).

Then verse 16 tells us, "And it shall come to pass, that every one that is left of all the nations which came against Jerusalem shall even go up from year to year to worship the King, the Lord of hosts, and to keep the feast of tabernacles." In that day Jerusalem will reach her destiny and her promised glory! With saved Israel, living in their own blessed, happy land, again a land flowing with milk and honey, the Lord Jesus shall rule, and we are told that

"In that day shall there be upon the bells of the horses, HO-LINESS UNTO THE LORD; and the pots in the Lord's house shall be like the bowls before the altar. Yea, every pot in Jerusalem and in Judah shall be holiness unto the Lord of hosts."
—Zech. 14:20, 21.

It becomes clear to the dullest mind, if it be opened to spiritual meaning at all, that God's promises to Israel are literal. The promises about the land of Canaan are literal. The promises about Jerusalem, or Mount Zion, are literal. Literal Israel according to the flesh will be brought back to their own land and there gloriously converted. Christ, the great Seed of David, will sit on David's literal throne in the literal city Jerusalem. What a glorious kingdom is coming!

The New Jerusalem on the New Earth to Be at the Same Site

For a thousand years we are told that Christ will reign in person on the earth before He shall turn the kingdom over to His Father (Rev. 20:4; Rev. 5:9, 10; I Cor. 15:24). In the judgment that will follow on this earth, every disease germ, every thorn and thistle, and every mark and remnant of sin must be utterly destroyed by fire. God has purposes for this planet that cannot be fulfilled as long as one sinner sets foot upon it, as long as a single mark of the curse remains upon it. Second Peter 3:10–13 tells how "the heavens shall pass away with a great noise, and the elements shall melt with fervent heat, the earth also and the works that are therein shall be burned up." In that holocaust the present heavens, or firmament, will be changed, and everything that fire can destroy will be destroyed, while the entire human race is present, out in space, at the judgment of sinners ("in the day of judgment and perdition of ungodly men").

But we have seen that God cannot do away with the elements that make up this world. He has promised to Abraham and his seed forever the land Palestine. He has set His name perpetually and forever at the place of the temple in Jerusalem. The temple has been destroyed three different times, and at least one other is to be built and fall; but God's name is placed at Jerusalem, His eyes are over it, His heart is centered upon it forever, as He Himself said (I Kings 9:3; II Chron. 7:16). The land must be made fertile and inhabited again, and God Himself has promised to plant it again like the Garden of Eden. Ezekiel 36:33–35 says:

"Thus saith the Lord God; In the day that I shall have cleansed you from all your iniquities I will also cause you to dwell in the cities, and the wastes shall be builded. And the desolate land shall be tilled, whereas it lay desolate in the sight of all that passed by. And they shall say, This land that was desolate is become like the garden of Eden; and the waste and desolate and ruined cities are become fenced, and are inhabited."

But what about Jerusalem? As God will make out of the old material a new earth, so God will provide a new Jerusalem. No sooner does God tell us about the new Heaven and the new earth, than God inspired John to tell of that new city Jerusalem which God will bring down and place where He has placed His name forever! In Revelation 21:1–3 we are taught that

"And I saw a new heaven and a new earth: for the first heaven and the first earth were passed away; and there was no more sea. And I John saw the holy city, new Jerusalem, coming down from God out of heaven, prepared as a bride adorned for her husband. And I heard a great voice out of heaven saying, Behold, the tabernacle of God is with men, and he will dwell with them, and they shall be his people, and God himself shall be with him, and be their God."

The New Jerusalem is the Father's house of many mansions of which Jesus spoke in John 14:2! This marvelous city, the home of God Himself, will be brought down to earth to be literally another Jerusalem at the place which God chose thousands of years ago. All of God's promises about Jerusalem will be fulfilled. The promises are literal—they will be fulfilled in a literal city, a literal Jerusalem on a literal earth, in the literal land of Palestine. Then God the Father, Himself, as well as the Son, will be King, in "the city of the great King."

There are some who teach that the New Jerusalem, that great city of God twelve thousand furlongs square, is simply to hover above the earth. Some teach that this heavenly Jerusalem will be inhabited by those converted in this gospel age which they call "the church," and that the earth will be inhabited by the Jews. But the Bible makes no distinction.

In the first place, that heavenly city is really "the new Jerusalem." When Chicago was destroyed in the great Chicago fire, a new Chicago was built on the site of the old Chicago. Jericho was destroyed by the children of Israel when they entered the land of Canaan. Later a new Jericho was built on the site of the old Jericho. So the New Jerusalem will be really Jerusalem, and on the site of the old Jerusalem. It must be a city on the earth, then. When the Apostle John on the Isle of Patmos was shown "that great city, the holy Jerusalem, descending out of heaven from God" (Rev. 21:10), he evidently saw that city as coming down to rest upon the earth and to be literally a new city Jerusalem at the ancient site. The ancient site itself is sacred. God's promises refer continually to "Mount Zion," and to "this place," and throughout Bible prophecy, Jerusalem is regarded as one eternal city, to be destroyed and then rebuilt, but continuing to inherit the same blessed promises.

Actually the New Jerusalem, that wonderful city described in detail in Revelation, chapters 21 and 22, will be the capital city of the new earth when it is purged from every taint and stain and mark of sin and disease and death. Christ Himself must reign there, sitting on David's throne. And we who suffer with Him shall also reign with Him on the earth.

Chapter 10

World-Wide Righteousness, Peace and Prosperity Promised in Christ's Kingdom

IN THE FIRST chapter of this book we set out to find the answers to certain great questions. The second question was: "Will this war-torn world ever have a real, permanent, world-wide peace?" The third question was: "Will the curse placed on this world because of sin ever be removed so that man can live here in a new Garden of Eden?" This chapter will answer these questions. During the reign of Christ on earth, the curse brought on nature because of sin will be removed. Wars will be no more, righteousness will prevail on the entire planet, and happiness will be universal.

This wonderful era, this golden age, will be on this literal planet, the earth. We are not talking about Heaven, except in the sense that Heaven will be on this earth as it certainly will. In previous chapters we have proved that the kingdom of Christ will be set up on this earth and that He will reign on David's throne, and now we want to discuss the happy conditions that will prevail in that golden age.

Animal Nature Changed; Gentle Lions!

We have called attention before to the promise of the Messiah's kingdom as given in Isaiah, chapter 11. There we were told in verse 1 that "there shall come forth a rod out of the stem of Jesse, and a Branch shall grow out of his roots." Verses 2 to 5 tell of the wisdom, justice and judgment of His reign on the earth. Then verses 6 to 9 tell us how even the nature of animals

will be changed until a little child can lead the wolf, the leopard
or the lion.

*"The wolf also shall dwell with the lamb, and the leopard
shall lie down with the kid; and the calf and the young lion and
the fatling together; and a little child shall lead them. And the
cow and the bear shall feed; their young ones shall lie down together: and the lion shall eat straw like the ox. And the sucking
child shall play on the hole of the asp, and the weaned child
shall put his hand on the cockatrice' den. They shall not hurt
nor destroy in all my holy mountain: for the earth shall be full
of the knowledge of the Lord, as the waters cover the sea. And in
that day there shall be a root of Jesse, which shall stand for an
ensign of the people; to it shall the Gentiles seek: and his rest
shall be glorious."*—Isa. 11:6–10.

What a great change in animal nature! The wolf, leopard and
young lion will no longer be beasts of prey and will do no harm
to the lamb, the kid and the fat calf. A child can play, in that
day, with the beasts of the field, as he might today with a puppy.
There will be no more carnivorous beasts, but "the lion shall eat
straw like the ox"! Babies may play with poisonous snakes with
no danger of harm, during the blessed kingdom of Jesus on
this earth!

How like the Garden of Eden that will be! At that time God
brought every fowl and beast to Adam "to see what he would
call them" (Gen. 2:19). We cannot imagine that animals in the
Garden of Eden were enemies of mankind, and there is no hint
in the Bible that animals were ever wild until God said to the
snake, "Thou art cursed above all cattle, and above every beast
of the field," and "I will put enmity between thee and the woman, and between thy seed and her seed" (Gen. 3:14, 15). The
snake was cursed "above all cattle;" that certainly means that
all cattle and beasts were cursed because of man's sin but that
the snake was cursed more. When Jesus comes to take charge
of the earth, the curse on animal nature will be removed. We
may be sure that that change will reach even to insects and disease
germs. If the lion will eat straw like the ox, and wolves, leopards,
and poisonous snakes will be safe playmates for the babies, we
may be sure that people in that happy time will be safe from the

sting of insects, from infection and bacteria or from harm by any of God's creatures.

Isaiah is full of glowing promises of the kingdom age. In chapter 65, verse 25, the prophet tells us again how the nature of animals and men will be changed in that day. "The wolf and the lamb shall feed together, and the lion shall eat straw like the bullock: and dust shall be the serpent's meat. They shall not hurt nor destroy in all my holy mountain, saith the Lord" (Isa. 65:25). Even if "dust shall be the serpent's meat" in that day, no animal will hurt nor destroy "in all my holy mountain," says the Lord.

The Curse on the Ground Removed

The saddest day this world ever saw was when the serpent of sin first put its slimy head in the Garden of Eden and led away from God Adam and Eve and with them all mankind. Because of this sin, animal life was cursed and then all the ground was cursed. We are told in Genesis 3:17,18:

"And unto Adam he said, Because thou hast hearkened unto the voice of thy wife, and hast eaten of the tree, of which I commanded thee, saying, Thou shalt not eat of it: cursed is the ground for thy sake; in sorrow shalt thou eat of it all the days of thy life; Thorns also and thistles shall it bring forth to thee; and thou shalt eat the herb of the field."

Since that curse on the ground, thorns and thistles have made life miserable for mankind. Animal life and plant life alike on the earth are against man. There is a curse on nature itself so that "the whole creation groaneth and travaileth in pain together until now" (Rom. 8:22), because of the curse of sin. This is the reason for storms, hail, floods, drought, barren land and deserts. For an illustration, the land of Palestine was once a land 'flowing with milk and honey' (Num. 13:27). Giant cedars of Lebanon were in Palestine, and the grapes of Eshcol were so fine that a bunch had to be carried between two men on a staff (Num. 13:23). It was a well watered, rich and happy land. But sin has brought a curse upon it. The soil has eroded. The trees have been cut down. The springs of water and brooks have dried up. Some of the land is desert and much of it is semi-arid. But the Holy Land will not remain under a curse, for the Lord has promised Israel that they should be brought back to their land and the land should be blessed again. Ezekiel 36:29, 30 says:

"I will also save you from all your uncleannesses: and I will call for the corn, and will increase it, and lay no famine upon you. And I will multiply the fruit of the tree, and the increase of the field, that ye shall receive no more reproach of famine among the heathen."

Then verse 35 in the same chapter says, "And they shall say, This land that was desolate is become like the garden of Eden." In some sense, the curse will be removed from all the earth, but more especially will that be true, it seems, in lovely Palestine; and it will become a veritable garden of the Lord.

In Isaiah, all of chapter 35 tells of the wonderful transformation of the earth, particularly Palestine and Jerusalem during the reign of Christ.

"The wilderness and the solitary place shall be glad for them; and the desert shall rejoice, and blossom as the rose. 2 It shall blossom abundantly, and rejoice even with joy and singing: the glory of Lebanon shall be given unto it, the excellency of Carmel and Sharon, they shall see the glory of the Lord, and the excellency of our God. 3 Strengthen ye the weak hands, and confirm the feeble knees. 4 Say to them that are of a fearful heart, Be strong, fear not: behold, your God will come with vengeance, even God with a recompence; he will come and save you. 5 Then the eyes of the blind shall be opened, and the ears of the deaf shall be unstopped. 6 Then shall the lame man leap as an hart, and the tongue of the dumb sing: for in the wilderness shall waters break out, and streams in the desert. 7 And the parched ground shall become a pool, and the thirsty land springs of water: in the habitation of dragons, where each lay, shall be grass with reeds and rushes. 8 And an highway shall be there, and a way, and it shall be called The way of holiness; the unclean shall not pass over it; but it shall be for those: the wayfaring men, though fools, shall not err therein. 9 No lion shall be there, nor any ravenous beast shall go up thereon, it shall not be found there; but the redeemed shall walk there: 10 And the ransomed of the Lord shall return, and come to Zion with songs and everlasting joy upon their heads:

they shall obtain joy and gladness, and sorrow and sighing shall flee away."

Even the earth itself will "be glad," "the desert shall rejoice, and blossom as the rose" in this kingdom of Christ on earth.

It is important to see that these passages are to be taken literally. If the first Garden of Eden was literal, so the second will be literal. If the trees and animals of the Garden of Eden were literal, then will these be literal in the kingdom of Christ on earth. Notice the names of literal places, "Lebanon," "Carmel," "Sharon." Zion, in verse 10, to which the ransomed of the Lord shall return with songs and everlasting joy, is the literal Mount Zion upon which the city Jerusalem rests. The water that shall break out in the wilderness and streams in the desert (verse 6) reminds us of the "river, the streams whereof shall make glad the city of God" (Psalm 46:4), which we discussed in the chapter on Jerusalem.

The wonderful blessings of Isaiah 35 will not come to pass until it can be said to them of fearful heart, "Be strong, fear not: behold, your God will come with vengeance, even God with a recompence; he will come and save you" (verse 4). This is the return of Christ to establish His kingdom when "he shall smite the earth with the rod of his mouth, and with the breath of his lips shall he slay the wicked" (Isa. 11:4).

The Curse Removed From Human Bodies, Too

It makes us happy to know that all nature will be glad, that the curse will be removed from beasts and from the earth itself. But happier still is the thought here expressed—that when Jesus returns to reign, the curse will be removed from our poor human bodies! Isaiah 35:5, 6 tells us that "then the eyes of the blind shall be opened, and the ears of the deaf shall be unstopped. Then shall the lame man leap as an hart, and the tongue of the dumb sing."

Read verse 10 of the same chapter and see the redeemed hosts of the Lord coming to Jerusalem at the beginning of the kingdom! "And the ransomed of the Lord shall return, and come to Zion with songs and everlasting joy upon their heads: they shall obtain joy and gladness, and sorrow and sighing shall flee away." No lame people! No blind, no dumb, no unmusical, and thank God, no sad people will live in the lovely city Jerusalem in that happy and prosperous reign of Christ.

The Sunday before this was written in Dallas, Texas, there joined our congregation an old man who is stone deaf. Though he sat near the front, he could not understand what I said. He felt the presence of God. He rejoiced when sinners came. But only the loudest noise can pierce into the silence of his mind. But in that happy kingdom, the Spirit tells us that "the ears of the deaf shall be unstopped" and my brother will hear again!

Today some women went to see Mother Lindsey. She is infirm and palsied and blind. She has heard me preach many times on the radio, and today she wept as she told the visiting ladies that she longed to see me and wondered what I looked like. She prays to live long enough and be well enough to come to join our church and be present in person in our services. But even then, she will have to be carried or led, for she cannot see. But in the reign of Christ, we are told that "the eyes of the blind shall be opened," and Mother Lindsey will see again.

World-Wide Righteousness

Sin is responsible for all the trouble in this world and sin brought the curse of God on man and beast and plants of the field. If the curse is to be removed from these in the kingdom age, then we know that it will be because of righteousness. It will be a happy, peaceful, and prosperous age because a righteous one.

The people of the earth will never be righteous unless they know the Lord. True righteousness is godliness. There can be no true morality without true religion. Christ is the Light of the world and the world will never be light until His light shines to every corner of the globe. People must know about God and know God through Jesus Christ before there can ever be any world-wide righteousness. This, we are told, will be true in the happy kingdom age.

The Scriptures tell us that the knowledge of the Lord shall cover the whole earth during the reign of Christ. Isaiah 11:9 says: "They shall not hurt nor destroy in all my holy mountain: for the earth shall be full of the knowledge of the Lord, as the waters cover the sea." The accompanying verses tell us that will be in a day when the great root of Jesse and Branch of David shall come and regather Israel and rule on the earth. The knowledge of the Lord will be everywhere.

A similar statement is found in Habakkuk 2:14: "For the earth shall be filled with the knowledge of the glory of the Lord, as the waters cover the sea."

Satan Will Be Chained During Kingdom Age

With all the preaching and teaching of nearly two thousand years, the earth has not yet been filled with the knowledge of the Lord. Bibles have been printed by the millions, and thousands of missionaries have spent their years all the way from Greenland's icy mountains to India's coral strand telling the story of Jesus. Multitudes have learned about the Lord, and many have been saved by His power, but we must admit that even yet there are multiplied millions in the earth today who know nothing of God, of His Son Jesus Christ, nor of the Bible, God's Word. Why the terrible spiritual darkness that covers the earth in spite of all the good gospel agencies? The answer is given in one word, Satan! The prince of darkness blinds the eyes of the people, stops their ears, hardens their hearts. The enemy sows tares among the wheat, puts leaven in the meal and makes the pure seed of the gospel into a denominational tree of human organization which becomes the home of wicked birds of unbelief. This world today is in darkness because Satan, the god of this world, makes it dark.

Then if the knowledge of the Lord is to cover the earth as the waters cover the sea, Satan must have his influence stopped that the light may shine on human hearts. And that is exactly what the Bible says will happen.

In Revelation 20:1-3 the story is told:

"And I saw an angel come down from heaven, having the key of the bottomless pit and a great chain in his hand. And he laid hold on the dragon, that old serpent, which is the Devil and Satan, and bound him a thousand years, And cast him into the bottomless pit, and shut him up, and set a seal upon him, that he should deceive the nations no more, till the thousand years should be fulfilled: and after that he must be loosed a little season."

This immediately follows the return of Christ in glory to destroy the armies of the wicked and to set up His kingdom, as told in Revelation, chapter 19. Thus at the beginning of the kingdom of Christ on earth, Satan will be bound and shut up in the bottomless pit "that he should deceive the nations no more, till the thousand years should be fulfilled." Of the thousand years, and of the loosing of Satan for a little season, we will speak in another chapter. But mark well that the golden age of world-wide righteousness, peace, and prosperity will be made possible because the Lord will shut up Satan. Then the knowledge of the Lord shall cover the earth.

Do not misunderstand me. The Bible does not say that every person alive on the earth during the kingdom age will be a Christian. A study of Revelation, chapter 20, will show that some unsaved people will live on through the thousand years, unsaved. At the close of the thousand years, when Satan is released, he will cause them to rebel; but until that time they will live in morality and without rebellion against God, submitting outwardly, at least, to His laws.

Jerusalem Will Be the Center of Worship and Knowledge for the Whole Earth

The prophet Micah, too, was inspired to tell of the kingdom of Christ on earth. The fourth chapter of Micah tells of that happy day, and verses 1 and 2 read:

"But in the last days it shall come to pass, that the mountain of the house of the Lord shall be established in the top of the mountains, and it shall be exalted above the hills; and people shall flow unto it. And many nations shall come, and say, Come, and let us go up to the mountain of the Lord, and to the house of the God of Jacob; and he will teach us of his ways, and we will walk in his paths: for the law shall go forth of Zion, and the word of the Lord from Jerusalem."

Jerusalem, Mount Zion, will be the center of worship, "for the law shall go forth of Zion, and the word of the Lord from Jerusalem." People all over the world will say, "Come, and let us go up to the mountain of the Lord, and to the house of the God of Jacob [the temple]; and he will teach us of his ways, and we will walk in his paths." Jerusalem will never fulfill its destiny until it is really the center of the earth.

The people who come up to Jerusalem will once a year keep the feast of tabernacles. And those Gentiles scattered throughout the earth who do not come to Jerusalem to worship Jesus, "the King, the Lord of hosts," on them there shall be no rain. That is what Zechariah 14:16, 17 tells us.

"And it shall come to pass, that every one that is left of all the nations which came against Jerusalem shall even go up from year to year to worship the King, the Lord of hosts, and to keep the feast of tabernacles. And it shall be, that whoso will not come up of all the families of the earth unto Jerusalem to worship the King, the Lord of hosts, even upon them shall be no rain."

The reign of Christ on earth will be a reign of righteousness, a spiritual reign, and the knowledge of the Lord will cover the whole earth.

All Israel Will Know the Lord

Among the Gentile nations of the earth, as we have said, it is evident that some will be unsaved, but nominally will serve the Lord without rebellion while Satan is chained. But among the Jews and at Jerusalem everyone will be devout and sincere children of God. Paul said concerning this time, "And so all Israel shall be saved" (Rom. 11:26). Elsewhere we will discuss the time of the marvelous conversion of all Israel. But now it is enough to notice that during the reign of Christ all Jews left alive will be Christian Jews as well as those saved Gentiles who will live with them near Christ in the Holy Land.

Jeremiah 31:33, 34 tells us how everyone of the house of Israel will have the law of God written in his heart and personally know the Lord in forgiven sins.

"But this shall be the covenant that I will make with the house of Israel; After those days, saith the Lord, I will put my law in their inward parts, and write it in their hearts; and will be their God, and they shall be my people. And they shall teach no more every man his neighbor, and every man his brother, saying, Know the Lord: for they shall all know me, from the least of them unto the greatest of them, saith the Lord: for I will forgive their iniquity, and I will remember their sin no more."—Jer. 31:33, 34.

The kingdom age will be an age of righteousness, with all the blessings that righteousness and godliness bring.

A Warless World

All that human education can do has never elevated mankind above strife and war. Peace treaties are scraps of paper. War grows more terrible with every invention of science, every centralization of government, every refinement of culture. Even Jesus Himself did not put a stop to war. Instead of that, He told how a few short years after His ascension Jerusalem would be utterly destroyed. And of the temple He said that "there shall not be left here one stone upon another, that shall not be thrown down" (Matt. 24:2). Of the course of this age, Jesus said that

"And ye shall hear of wars and rumors of wars: see that ye be not troubled: for all these things must come to pass, but the end is not yet. For nation shall rise against nation, and kingdom against kingdom: and there shall be famines, and pestilences, and earthquakes, in divers places. All these are the beginning of sorrows."—Matt. 24:6–8.

War! Pestilence! Famine! Earthquakes! These are the characteristics of this wicked age in which we live. The kingdom which is promised was not set up at the first coming of Christ, nor since that time; but for it we must look to the future when Christ shall come in power to reign, when with the last great battle He will make an end forever of wars. Wars and rumors of war curse this earth, cause rivers of blood and tears. The bitterness, the hate, and the crime of war have blasted the hopes, broken the bodies, snuffed out the lives and damned the souls of uncounted millions. But thank God, it will no longer be so in the kingdom of Christ on earth.

A bit ago we studied the first two verses of Micah, chapter 4. That is found almost word for word in Isaiah, chapter 2. The fourth chapter of Micah is a wonderful picture of the kingdom, and verse 7 says that "the Lord shall reign over them in mount Zion from henceforth, even for ever." The chapter certainly discusses, then, the reign of Christ on earth. Now let us read verses 3 and 4.

"And he shall judge among many people, and rebuke strong nations afar off; and they shall beat their swords into plowshares, and their spears into pruninghooks: nation shall not lift up a sword against nation, neither shall they learn war any more. But they shall sit every man under his vine and under his fig tree; and none shall make them afraid: for the mouth of the Lord of hosts hath spoken it."

Christ's Reign on David's Throne "According to the Flesh"

In Peter's sermon at Pentecost, he took occasion to mention, as he usually did, the resurrection of Christ and His position as the coming King of Israel. All the apostles knew that Jesus in the future would take His place as the King of Israel and sit on David's throne. They preached it again and again. They looked for that to occur at any time, just as they had been taught to watch continually for the second coming of Christ. In Acts 1:6, they had asked, "Lord, wilt thou AT THIS TIME restore again the kingdom to Israel?" and they were told that the time was not for them to know. In Acts 2:25-28, Peter quotes the sixteenth Psalm to prove the resurrection of Christ, and then explains it in Acts 2:29-31 as follows:

"Men and brethren, let me freely speak unto you of the patriarch David, that he is both dead and buried, and his sepulchre is with us unto this day. 30 Therefore being a prophet, and knowing that God had sworn with an oath to him, that of the fruit of his loins, according to the flesh, he would raise up Christ to sit on his throne; 31 He seeing this before spake of the resurrection of Christ, that his soul was not left in hell, neither his flesh did see corruption."

Notice verse 30. David knew God had sworn to him with an oath that "of the fruit of his loins, ACCORDING TO THE FLESH, he would raise up Christ to sit on his throne." The resurrection of Christ was primarily looking toward the reign of Christ. The resurrection was a bodily resurrection, "according to the flesh." "According to the flesh" Christ will sit on David's throne! The reign of Christ, then, will be a literal one. With His literal, physical body, the body with the nail prints in the hands, with the side that Thomas touched, with the feet that "shall stand in that day upon the mount of Olives" (Zech. 14:4), with the body that ate broiled fish and honeycomb before the disciples (Luke 24:42, 43), Christ will sit on the throne of David at Jerusalem and rule over the house of Jacob, as David did, except in a much greater fashion and with an everlasting kingdom! The kingdom of Christ on David's throne will be "ACCORDING TO THE FLESH." In the revised version, Acts 2:30 does not use the term "according to the flesh" but says: "Being therefore a prophet, and knowing that God had sworn with an oath to him, that of the fruit of his loins he would set one upon his throne."

The fact still stands out that Christ, in order to reign on David's throne, must be resurrected in the body. In the resurrection of Christ, God the Father primarily had this in mind, that Jesus should reign on David's throne. David had a human body when he reigned on his throne. His reign was a literal reign, a physical reign over subjects with physical bodies. So Christ, to sit on the throne of David, must have been raised from the dead with His glorified, human body.

Do you see how this proves the literal reign of Christ? His reign will be different from any reign that could be administered without a human body. Jesus before His coming in the flesh could not have reigned on David's throne. After His death, He could not have reigned on David's throne, in the way the Scriptures foretold, without a human body. He must be raised from the dead. The Scriptures about His reign would not be fulfilled if Christ should not reign on a throne over such subjects and in such a kingdom as involved a literal, resurrection, glorified, human body.

Chapter 11

The Saved and Glorified to Reign With Christ on Earth After His Coming

ERTAIN simple truths have become clear in your mind as you prayfully studied the Scriptures in the preceding chapters. Israel is to be regathered to Palestine as God promised to Abraham, Isaac, Jacob, David and the whole nation. A remnant of the race will be brought back alive to Palestine and be converted and will possess the land. With them will come the resurrected, saved Jews of past ages. Saved Gentiles, too, will come to live with Christ on the earth.

The kingdom of Israel will be restored again, and Christ will sit on the throne of His Father David and reign forever at Jerusalem. Jerusalem will be the joy of the whole earth.

Surely, if you believe the Bible, by this time you must be convinced that the reign of Christ will be a literal reign, on a literal earth, over a literal people with physical bodies, and on a literal throne. If the Bible means what it says, and if it can be taken at face value, then these promises are to be taken as true and understandable, and will be literally fulfilled.

Last but not least, in the preceding chapters it must have become clear that this wonderful era of peace and righteousness and joy, of the kingdom of Christ on earth, must follow the second coming of Christ. The King must come before His kingdom shall cover the earth.

Every Saved Soul in the Universe Will Be on This Earth

If Heaven is going to be on this earth, then we must expect that all the saved will be here, and that is true. Several Scriptures make clear that all the saved will be on the earth with Christ when He returns and rules over it in person.

First, all the saints, living and dead, will be changed and resurrected when Christ calls us into the air to meet Him. I Corinthians 15:51, 52 says:

"Behold, I shew you a mystery; We shall not all sleep, but we shall all be changed, In a moment, in the twinkling of an eye, at the last trump: for the trumpet shall sound, and the dead shall be raised incorruptible, and we shall be changed."

Here Paul is inspired to say plainly that though "we shall not all sleep" (die), yet "we shall ALL be changed." The book of First Corinthians is addressed to "all that in every place call upon the name of Jesus Christ our Lord, both their's and our's" (I Cor. 1:2). It is addressed to all the saved of all ages, and to these Paul says, "We shall ALL be changed." Every saved person then dead will be resurrected, and every saved person then living will be changed in a moment to meet Christ in the air.

In Hebrews 12:22–24 we have a picture of that assembled host, raptured, called up to meet Jesus in the air for our honeymoon in Heaven, before He begins His reign on earth. The "church" which is His body, all the redeemed, will be with Jesus at that time. Read the passage carefully and notice that the assembly is not a partial assembly but a "general assembly." Notice that that called-out assembly is composed of "the firstborn," those "which are written in heaven;" again, "the spirits of just men made perfect." That assembly in Heaven will surely include every person saved up to that time.

That happy occasion, so often called "the rapture," is also pictured in I Thessalonians 4:16, 17 as follows:

"For the Lord himself shall descend from heaven with a shout, with the voice of the archangel, and with the trump of God: and the dead in Christ shall rise first: Then we which are alive and remain shall be caught up together with them in the clouds, to meet the Lord in the air: and so shall we ever be with the Lord."

The dead in Christ shall rise first, not a part of them, but all of them. Then we that are alive and remain, not a part of us, but all of us, the saved, will be caught up together with them to meet the Lord in the air. No hint is made here of any who have ever been saved being left behind.

The Resurrected Saints Must Go Where Christ Goes

Now notice the concluding statement in verse 17, "so shall we EVER be with the Lord." From this time on, the saved are the bride of Christ. Where He goes, they will go. When He returns to reign on the earth, they will return to reign with Him. Not one of these saved people will ever any more have any real separation from Jesus Christ. That is one reason that that time is spoken of as a marriage. The Bridegroom will meet His bride. Sweethearts will become husband and wife. After that, they are yoked together; and in this case, what God has joined together man cannot put asunder. Christians will be with Jesus wherever He is from that time forth.

We have spoken here about the time when Christians will be called up into the air to meet Christ. There we will meet the Saviour and have the wedding supper. There we will be judged, each one at the judgment seat of Christ. (That will not be a judgment to determine whether we are saved or not, nor even to declare it. It will be a judgment to announce rewards for service, which will greatly vary.) During our time in Heaven with the Saviour, the terrible reign of the Antichrist will begin, cover the whole earth, and come to climactic ruin. And then the Saviour will return to this earth in person to set up His kingdom—*and we will come with Him.*

"The Lord My God Shall Come, and All the Saints With Thee"

In Zechariah the fourteenth chapter, the Holy Spirit gives us a clear picture of "the day of the Lord." That is the time when the Lord Jesus shall come into His own, when He shall defeat His enemies and establish His kingdom on the earth. That "day of the Lord" is mentioned many times throughout the Bible, and the term refers to the entire period from the setting up of Christ's kingdom on David's throne when Christ returns, through a thousand years' reign and until sinners are judged and the kingdom is turned over to the Father, after which Father and Son will reign together on the earth. The "day of the Lord" begins at the literal return of Christ to the earth to begin His reign.

The fourteenth chapter of Zechariah starts off with the statement, "Behold, the day of the Lord cometh," and then tells of all nations being gathered against Jerusalem to destroy it. In the midst of that destruction, verse 3 tells us, "Then shall the Lord go forth," and verse 4 says that "His feet shall stand in that day upon the mount of Olives." Then in verse 5 we are told, "And the Lord my God shall come, *and all the saints with thee.*" Following that, verse 9 tells us that "The Lord shall be king over all the earth."

When Jesus returns to reign, to be King over all the earth, then "ALL THE SAINTS" will return with Him. And with the living Jews, regathered to Palestine and converted, will be all the saints in the universe with Christ when He reigns on this earth. These saints will cover the earth, we understand, and will not all live in Palestine.

Tribulation Saints Will Be Here Too

During the tribulation time, while the church, that called-out assembly, is with the Saviour in Heaven, others will be converted here on this earth. Revelation 7:1–8 tells us of an hundred and forty-four thousand Israelites who will be converted during that time. In Revelation 14:1–4 we are given a vision of them again, standing on Mount Zion (at Jerusalem), and we are told that they are the "firstfruits." Evidently these Jews, converted during the Great Tribulation, are firstfruits in the sense that at the close of the tribulation, when the fulness of the Gentiles be come in, then "all Israel shall be saved" (Romans 11:24–26). So some Jews will be converted in the tribulation period, as firstfruits of the great revival among Jews.

In Revelation 7:9–14 we find a description of a great number of others who are not Jews, ". . . a great multitude, which no man could number, of all nations, and kindreds, and people, and tongues." Then in verse 14 we are told, "These are they which came out of great tribulation, and have washed their robes, and made them white in the blood of the Lamb." Here are tribulation saints, converted during the time of tribulation on earth when those of us who are now Christians will be at the wedding supper in Heaven. What will become of these Christians when Christ returns to reign on the earth? The answer is, they will reign with us and with Him. In the same chapter, verse 15 says about them, "And he that sitteth on the throne shall dwell among them," and verse 17 says that the Lamb "shall feed them, and shall lead them unto living fountains of waters." They too will be with Christ where He is when He returns to reign on the earth.

In Revelation, chapters 19 and 20, we have again a description of the return of Christ to reign on the earth, of the battle of Armageddon, and of the happy millennium. In Revelation 20, verse 4, we are told how even those put to death for Christ during that tribulation time will be resurrected to reign with Him.

"And I saw thrones, and they sat upon them, and judgment was given unto them: and I saw the souls of them that were beheaded for the witness of Jesus, and for the word of God, and which had not worshipped the beast, neither his image, neither had received his mark upon their foreheads, or in their hands; and they lived and reigned with Christ a thousand years."

Verses 5 and 6 after that tell us that the unsaved dead will not be raised until a thousand years later, but that all who are in the first resurrection shall reign with Christ.

"But the rest of the dead lived not again until the thousand years were finished. This is the first resurrection. Blessed and holy is he that hath part in the first resurrection: on such the second death hath no power, but they shall be priests of God and of Christ, and shall reign with him a thousand years."

"We Shall Reign on the Earth"—Rev. 5:10

It is hard for some people to believe that saints will reign with Christ on earth. So lest some should misunderstand and think the reign mentioned here will be in Heaven, it is well to go back to the fifth chapter of Revelation where we are expressly told that these saints will reign literally on the earth. The church age is pictured in Revelation, closing with the third chapter. The fourth chapter begins with the rapture of the saints, and soon afterward the book tells of the Great Tribulation. John was caught up into Heaven to behold a throne set in Heaven (Rev. 4:1, 2) and around the throne were beautiful living creatures (improperly translated beasts) which remind us of the cherubim and seraphim mentioned in the Old Testament. And around that throne were twenty-four elders. These twenty-four men are not named, but they say that they are simply redeemed men, redeemed by the blood of Christ from various nations on the earth. Now Revelation 5:8–10 tells us that these elders, then seen in Heaven with Christ, will reign on the earth.

"And when he had taken the book, the four beasts and four and twenty elders fell down before the Lamb, having every one of them harps, and golden vials full of odours, which are the prayers of saints. And they sung a new song, saying, Thou art worthy to take the book, and to open the seals thereof: for thou wast slain, and hast redeemed us to God by thy blood out of every kindred, and tongue, and people, and nation; And hast made us unto our God kings and priests: and we shall reign on the earth."

—Rev. 5:8–10.

In Revelation 5:9, 10 these elders said, "Thou . . . hast made us unto our God kings and priests: and we shall reign ON THE EARTH." Then Revelation 20:6 says, "Blessed and holy is he that hath part in the first resurrection: on such the second death hath no power, but they shall be priests of God and of Christ, and shall reign with him a thousand years." The reign of the saints is on the earth with Christ. These elders and all others who will be in the first resurrection, the resurrection of the saved, will reign on earth with Christ.

Again I am reminded that some people think that the heavenly Jerusalem will be hovering up above the world somewhere instead of coming down to the site of the present city Jerusalem. They think that Gentile Christians, including those saved in the present or church age, will live in the heavenly city up above the earth and perhaps in some fashion reign over the earth.

With this in mind, they call attention to the marginal reading of Revelation 5:10. By the word "on" is a reference letter, and in the margin of the Scofield Reference Bible we are told that the word "on" should be really "over." So we might translate the statement of these twenty-four elders of every kindred and tribe, "We shall reign *over* the earth" instead of "We shall reign *on* the earth."

It is true that the Greek word here could properly be translated "over," but it does not necessarily mean physically "above." In the Greek, as in the English, the word for "over" often refers to authority and not to physical position above. If I should speak of Hitler's rule over Europe, I would not mean that Hitler was suspended in the air over Europe, but rather that he exercised authority over Europe. Joseph Stalin rules over Russia, but that simply means that he has authority over Russia, not that he is hanging in the air somewhere over Russia.

So these twenty-four saints of God up in Heaven praising the Lord Jesus merely say that Christ has made them kings and priests, "and we shall reign *on the earth.*"

I remember that this was made clear in an article in *The Sunday School Times* by Dr. James Oliver Buswell.

Thus we see that the saints of God will literally be on the earth as Christ will be on the earth. He will reign from the throne of His father, David, at Jerusalem; the twelve apostles will sit on twelve thrones judging the twelve tribes of Israel; and Christians, on earth with Christ, will help Him reign. According to our Saviour, in the parable of the pounds, to one faithful Christian Christ will say, "Well, thou good servant: because thou hast been faithful in a very little, have thou authority over ten cities." And to another, "Be thou also over five cities" (Luke 19:17–19).

I find no Scriptural authority whatever for the idea that the New Jerusalem will be suspended up in the air and that it will be reserved for a favored group called "the church," while Jews will live on the earth. No, the great Bible teaching is, as I see it, that the New Jerusalem will be the capital city of the world. It will be, naturally, on Mount Zion, in Palestine, where Jerusalem has always been. And this city will be the center of the kingdom of Christ and of God. Saints of Christ will reign on the earth with Him.

You can see, then, that even the saints converted during the tribulation time will reign with Christ on the earth. Every saved soul in the universe will be on the earth with Christ during that time.

Two resurrections are mentioned in the verses we quoted above, in Revelation 20:4–6. The first resurrection is a resurrection of saved people only. Part of the first resurrection takes place at the rapture and the rest of the first resurrection takes place when Christ returns to reign and when the tribulation saints receive their resurrection bodies. The second resurrection is a thousand years later and will be composed of the unsaved alone. The twentieth chapter of Revelation will make this plain. The passages you have studied thus show that every Christian who ever died will be resurrected to reign with Christ on the earth, but that every lost sinner who ever died will still be in Hell and his body in the grave during the thousand years of Christ's reign on earth.

Literal Flesh and Bone Bodies

Strange it is how the Devil tries to make Christians believe that the promises of God are not literally true. Satan has made many people believe that Heaven is afar off, an unreal place of disembodied spirits. And Christians generally have been made to believe that in the resurrection we will not have literal bodies of flesh and bone and blood, bodies that eat and drink. This idea of the unreality of the future and of resurrection bodies is widespread. I am shocked when I hear the question over and over again, "Will we know our loved ones in Heaven?" That question shows how far wrong has been the teaching which most people have received on this question. I answer back that we certainly will know our loved ones. They will have physical bodies as real as the bodies they have now, and as far as we know, of the same size, and made out of the same materials and readily recognizable to the eye. Whatever mark of sin there is will be removed, but we will have literal, physical bodies, bodies with normal functions, bodies of flesh and bone, bodies that eat and drink.

"Will We Know Each Other in Heaven?"

Yes, we will know our loved ones in Heaven and when we come back to this earth to rule with Christ in a Heaven on this earth, not only will we know people's outward appearances and recognize our loved ones, but then we will know people's hearts even as God knows our hearts today. We will know even our most intimate loved ones far better than we have ever known them in this life.

On this matter, I Corinthians 13:12 says: "For now we see through a glass, darkly; but then face to face: now I know in part;

but then shall I know even as also I am known." Yes, we will know each other as Moses and Elijah and Jesus knew each other on the Mount of Transfiguration. We will know each other even as my mother on her death bed looked into Heaven and said, "I can see Jesus and my baby now." Now we see through a glass darkly. We see people's faces but not their hearts. We hear people's words but not the cry of their souls. We see what people accomplish; we do not see what they hoped for, but never did. God does see, and one day we shall see as He sees, and know as He knows, not looking through a glass darkly, but face to face, and we will know each other in Heaven, and on this earth.

The bodies of resurrected Christians will be like the resurrected body of Christ, and we are clearly told about what kind of body He had. In Luke 24:36–43 we are told how Jesus appeared to the apostles after His resurrection, and how He showed them what kind of a body He had.

"And as they thus spake, Jesus himself stood in the midst of them, and saith unto them, Peace be unto you. But they were terrified and affrighted, and supposed that they had seen a spirit. And he said unto them, Why are ye troubled? and why do thoughts arise in your hearts? Behold my hands and my feet, that it is I myself: handle me, and see; for a spirit hath not flesh and bones, as ye see me have. And when he had thus spoken, he shewed them his hands and his feet. And while they yet believed not for joy, and wondered, he said unto them, Have ye here any meat? And they gave him a piece of a broiled fish, and of an honeycomb. And he took it, and did eat before them."—Luke 24:36–43.

The resurrected Jesus was not just a spirit. Jesus had a spiritual body in the sense that it was not carnal, with the taint of sin. But it was a literal, physical body. In verse 39, Jesus said, "A spirit hath not flesh and bones, as ye see me have." The resurrected Jesus showed them that His was a body with flesh and bones. Jesus encouraged them to handle Him and see for themselves, and when they could scarcely believe Him for joy, He further proved the literalness of His physical, resurrection body by calling for food. Before them He ate a piece of broiled fish and part of an honeycomb.

I have heard preachers say that the resurrection body of Jesus is the kind of body that can go into a room when the door is shut. But I remind you, Jesus could always do that, even in the body He had from birth. That was not in the nature of the body, that was in the power of Christ. This was a physical body of flesh and bones, a body that ate and drank.

The Gospel of John tells us that Thomas was not with the disciples when Jesus first appeared on the day of His resurrection (John 20:24–29). He did not believe the words of the other disciples about the resurrected Saviour and said, "Except I shall see in his hands the print of the nails, and put my finger into the print of the nails, and thrust my hand into his side, I will not believe." But after eight days the Saviour came again and Thomas saw the print of the nails with his own eyes, and put his finger on those scars, and believed! So the resurrection body of Jesus was simply the old body glorified and made new. He had the same features, though glorified. He had the same wounds in His hands and in His side. It was a literal, physical body which Jesus had after His resurrection.

The Same Jesus With the Same Body Will Come Again

When Jesus comes again to the earth to reign, He will have that same glorified, resurrection body with which He went away. In the first chapter of Acts we are told about the ascension of the Saviour. Read Acts 1:9–11 with me and see that Jesus is coming back with the same body in which He went away.

"And when he had spoken these things, while they beheld, he was taken up; and a cloud received him out of their sight. And while they looked stedfastly toward heaven as he went up, behold, two men stood by them in white apparel; Which also said, Ye men of Galilee, why stand ye gazing up into heaven? this same Jesus, which is taken up from you into heaven, shall so come in like manner as ye have seen him go into heaven."

This Scripture is to be taken literally. Jesus went away into Heaven and the angels said, "This same Jesus" will return again. It is remarkable how many details of Christ's ascension will be duplicated at His Second Coming. For instance, Acts 1:12 tells us that the ascension was from the Mount of Olives or Olivet. Zechariah 14:4 tells us that at His coming, "His feet shall stand in that day upon the mount of Olives." As He went away, Acts 1:9 tells us, "A cloud received him out of their sight." His return to reign will be with clouds also, for Revelation 1:7 tells us, "Behold, he cometh with clouds; and every eye shall see him." Matthew 24:30 tells us that "They shall see the Son of man coming in the clouds of heaven." His ascension was visible, and His return to reign will be visible. His ascension was that of a physical body, His return will be that of a physical body. He stood on the Mount of Olives before He went away, and His feet shall return to that place when He comes in glory. A cloud received Him out of their sight, and behold He cometh with clouds! It is the same Jesus, the Jesus with a resurrected body, the Jesus who ate and drank before them who shall come again to the earth.

It was this that Jesus had in mind when He gave the Last Supper and said to His disciples in Matthew 26:29, "But I say unto you, I will not drink henceforth of this fruit of the vine, until that day when I drink it new with you in my Father's kingdom."

Our Bodies Like His Body

Now comes the happy thought that the bodies of the saved will be like the body of Jesus, that is, a literal body of flesh and bones and blood when we live with Him on this earth after His coming.

At the first resurrection, Christians will receive glorified bodies. When Jesus comes into the air to receive His saints, the trumpet shall sound and "we shall all be changed." Then the mortal bodies will put on immortality, then corruption will put on incorruption. Then our bodies will be like Jesus' body. Philippians 3:20, 21 tells of this blessed hope of a Christian.

"For our conversation is in heaven; from whence also we look for the Saviour, the Lord Jesus Christ: Who shall change our vile body, that it may be fashioned like unto his glorious body, according to the working whereby he is able even to subdue all things unto himself."

Our vile bodies will be changed, and "fashioned like unto his glorious body" when Jesus raises and changes His saints and calls us to meet Him in the air. So whatever kind of body Jesus had after His resurrection, the kind He has now, that will be the kind of body we will have as we reign with Christ and enjoy the bless-ings of God in a Heaven on earth.

That is what Jesus meant in the verse quoted above, Matthew 26:29, where He said, "But I say unto you, I will not drink hence-forth of this fruit of the vine, until that day when I drink it new with you in my Father's kingdom."

Jesus said, "I will drink it new WITH YOU." Jesus will drink grape juice in His kingdom on earth and will eat and drink as He did when He appeared to His disciples after His resurrection. And praise God for the thought, we will have bodies like His and will drink grape juice with Him in the happy kingdom which the Father will give to Him on this earth!

Some one will quote I Corinthians 15:50, "Flesh and blood can-not inherit the kingdom of God," as evidence that we will not have literal bodies of flesh and blood in the kingdom age. But I remind you that Jesus Himself has already said that He had flesh and bones and was not just a spirit, and we will find how the same Jesus is coming back again and how Christians will have bodies like unto His glorious body. To be sure, flesh and blood cannot inherit the kingdom. If that is all it took, then every descendant of Abraham would be in the kingdom. But the promise is by faith, and not just by flesh and blood. It is not just a kingdom inherited by natural bodies according to a fleshly birth. The in-heritance of this kingdom is based on a new birth and not on the first birth. That is what the Holy Spirit evidently meant in I Corinthians 15:50. Flesh and blood cannot inherit the kingdom, that is true; but glorified flesh and blood certainly will be in the kingdom, inherited by saved souls.

Some good people teach that resurrected bodies will have flesh and bones but no blood. The Bible never says so. But when the apostles eat and drink at Christ's table in His kingdom, as He has said they shall (Luke 22:30), and when He drinks with them grape juice in this kingdom (Matthew 26:29), then certainly the human body will have liquid in it, and the digestive processes will be carried on. If one objects that the blood of Jesus was poured out on the cross, why, of course that is true. But He also poured out His soul unto death (Isa. 53:12). But God would not leave His soul in the place of the dead nor leave His dead body to see corruption, and the same miracle that brought again Jesus

Christ from the dead and raised that body into a glorified body could restore the blood as well as the flesh and spirit. I beg you, my Christian people, take the Bible at face value and believe that we will have literal bodies of flesh and bones and blood, bodies that eat and drink, bodies that we will recognize, and yet sinless and strong and glorious, in the kingdom of Christ on earth.

"The Lame Man Shall Leap As an Hart, and the Tongue of the Dumb Shall Sing"

In Isaiah, chapter 35, we have a glorious description of the earth and mankind during the kingdom age. "The wilderness and the solitary place shall be glad for them; and the desert shall rejoice, and blossom as the rose" then, we are told. Evidently the curse of sin on this earth will be removed and there will be no more droughts, pestilences, thorns, and thistles as the consequence of man's sin. At least those evils will be under control, though we are told in Zechariah 14:17, 18 that temporary droughts may be permitted during that time as a disciplinary measure. But the land of Palestine will have the curse removed and the ransomed of the Lord shall return, and sorrow and sighing shall flee away.

In that chapter we are also told that the curse will be removed from the resurrection bodies of the saved. Isaiah 35:5, 6 says: "Then the eyes of the blind shall be opened, and the ears of the deaf shall be unstopped. Then shall the lame man leap as an hart, and the tongue of the dumb sing." These verses teach that we will have bodies with literal eyes that see, literal ears that hear, that we will really leap and sing. These are the functions of a physical body. But even better than that is the teaching that we will have perfect bodies. Blindness, deafness, lameness, and dumbness will all be corrected in our resurrection bodies. Whatever of frailty and weakness we suffer now, there will come a good time when it will be removed, thank God!

These verses indicate that all the saved will have resurrected bodies. In the rapture, when the first part of the first resurrection takes place, we are plainly told that "the dead shall be raised incorruptible, and we shall be changed," so all those who are saved up until that time, *the living as well as the dead,* will be given resurrection bodies. Then Revelation 20:4 tells us that the tribulation saints, put to death because of their faith in Christ, will be resurrected. Certainly we would expect those saved during the tribulation period who remain alive when Jesus returns to the earth to reign to be changed likewise at that time. And Isaiah 35:5, 6 indicates that that will be true. All the saved will have glorified bodies with no blind or dumb or deaf or lame.

The perfect health which God will give His people during that period will be blessed. Isaiah 33:24 says: "And the inhabitant shall not say, I am sick: the people that dwell therein shall be forgiven their iniquity." With sins forgiven, then the disease that follows sin will be conquered and people will no more say, "I am sick," but will rejoice in the perfect use of eyes, ears, limbs and voice to the glory of God.

Food During the Kingdom Age

Jesus made clear that the saved will eat and drink with Him in the coming kingdom (Luke 22:30, Matthew 26:29). Where will the food come from? Will the earth bring forth crops as it does now? Evidently it will, only without the limitations of drought, insect pests, thorns and thistles, which came upon the earth as a curse because of man's sin. Plants will grow, much more as they did in the Garden of Eden than as they do now.

In Ezekiel, chapter 47, a wonderful river of water is pictured flowing out from the sanctuary of the temple in Jerusalem. We are told that trees bearing "new fruit according to his months" shall grow on either side of this river that shall make glad the city of God. The same passage tells how half the river will flow out to the Mediterranean Sea and half of it will flow into the Dead Sea and the salt water will be healed so that there will be fish in the Dead Sea as there is fish now in the Mediterranean Sea. Read Ezekiel 47:7-12 and see about some of the food of the kingdom age.

"Now when I had returned, behold, at the bank of the river were very many trees on the one side and on the other. Then said he unto me, These waters issue out toward the east country, and go down into the desert, and go into the sea: which being brought forth into the sea, the waters shall be healed. And it shall come to pass, that every thing that liveth, which moveth, whithersoever the rivers shall come, shall live: and there shall be a very great

multitude of fish, because these waters shall come thither: for they shall be healed; and every thing shall live whither the river cometh. And it shall come to pass, that the fishers shall stand upon it from En-gedi even unto En-eglaim; they shall be a place to spread forth nets; their fish shall be according to their kinds, as the fish of the great sea, exceeding many. But the miry places thereof and the marishes thereof shall not be healed; they shall be given to salt. And by the river upon the bank thereof, on this side and on that side, shall grow all trees for meat, whose leaf shall not fade, neither shall the fruit thereof be consumed: it shall bring forth new fruit according to his months, because their waters they issued out of the sanctuary: and the fruit thereof shall be for meat, and the leaf thereof for medicine."

It seems clear that the people in the land of Palestine at least will eat fish from the Dead Sea and have them salted with salt from the marishes thereof. Certainly the fruit of the trees will be food also. Doubtless, every wonderful food the earth had in the Garden of Eden will be here again. This is a kingdom of literal people with literal bodies, bodies that eat and drink. We may be sure that all the saved, resurrected and glorified, will have the same kind of bodies.

Chapter 12

Some Unsaved, on Earth, in Natural Bodies, During Millennium

HERE WE ARE come to a rather difficult question. Will there be unsaved people on this earth during the millennium, the thousand-years reign of Christ? The answer unquestionably is, Yes. Strange as it may seem, during the millennium, that first thousand years of Christ's reign before the Father comes down and the New Jerusalem from Heaven, this earth will have sinners on it. Several Scriptures prove that this is so.

For example, Isaiah 65:20 says: "There shall be no more thence an infant of days, nor an old man that hath not filled his days: for the child shall die an hundred years old; but the sinner being an hundred years old shall be accursed." "The SINNER being an hundred years old shall be accursed." That Scripture certainly indicates in that time of rejoicing and joy in Jerusalem, yet there will be sinners on the earth. However, if there is yet doubt, turn to Revelation the twentieth chapter. There we are told how Satan will be chained and shut up for a thousand years "that he should deceive the nations no more, till the thousand years shall be fulfilled." The blessed reign of peace for a thousand years is described with Christ reigning, and His saints with Him, over the entire earth. Then we are told how Satan will be loosed out of his prison and will deceive the nations again, bringing them even to open rebellion against God. As you read that chapter, you will become convinced that on the earth during the thousand years there will be unsaved sinners, certainly some lost people without resurrection bodies. Read Revelation 20, verses 1–3, and verses 7–8.

*"And I saw an angel come down from heaven, having the key
of the bottomless pit and a great chain in his hand. And he laid
hold on the dragon, that old serpent, which is the Devil, and
Satan, and bound him a thousand years, And cast him into the
bottomless pit, and shut him up, and set a seal upon him, that he
should deceive the nations no more, till the thousand years shall
be fulfilled: and after that he must be loosed a little season."*

*"And when the thousand years are expired, Satan shall be
loosed out of his prison, And shall go out to deceive the nations
which are in the four quarters of the earth, Gog and Magog, to
gather them together to battle: the number of whom is as the sand
of the sea."*

It is clear that Satan will be bound because there will be people
on the earth whom he might deceive during the thousand years.
I do not believe he would be likely to deceive glorified, perfected
Christians. But Satan is chained and shut up in the bottomless pit
until the close of the thousand years. During that time the Scriptures make clear there will be no open rebellion against God.
Whatever weakness there is by nature in man's heart, it will not
break out into vicious and open sin. The occasion is lacking.
Satan himself, during that thousand years, will be shut up away
from mankind. This proves a personal Devil who deceives individuals and leads them to sin.

But at the close of the thousand years, we are told that Satan
will be released and will deceive the nations again. We are told
that Satan shall deceive the nations which are in the four quarters
of the earth, and so set them against Christ that they will gather
armies as the sand of the sea for multitudes against Jerusalem,
the Holy City. Then we are told that fire will come down from
God out of Heaven and devour them. It is unthinkable that saved
people, made perfect, and with glorified bodies, could be so deceived that they would be brought to fight against Christ in person. Such open and wicked rebellion against Christ, such seeking
even to destroy Christ and His kingdom, would prove that those
who take part in the rebellion are not glorified Christians, to say
the least. This is the act of unsaved sinners in natural bodies.
Their end is destruction, and the Scripture tells us that they will

be destroyed by fire from God out of Heaven. This again is proof that they are not glorified saints. It seems certain that a glorified saint will never sin. It seems also certain that a glorified body will never be destroyed. When that which is mortal puts on immortality (I Cor. 15:53) and corruptible put on incorruption, then the body will be as incorruptible and as immortal as the soul, and God will not bring fire down from Heaven and destroy His glorified saints. No, these rebels are unsaved men on the earth who will be kept in strict subjection during the thousand years while Satan is chained. Then when Satan is loosed for a season, he will deceive them and bring them to an open and violent rebellion against God and Christ.

Zechariah 14:16–18 indicates that there shall be some left of the nations of the earth who will be unsaved, and shows how God will keep them disciplined and in strict obedience during the thousand years.

"And it shall come to pass, that every one that is left of all the nations which came against Jerusalem shall even go up from year to year to worship the King, the Lord of hosts, and to keep the feast of tabernacles. And it shall be, that whoso will not come up of all the families of the earth unto Jerusalem to worship the King, the Lord of hosts, even upon them shall be no rain. And if the family of Egypt go not up, and come not, that have no rain; there shall be the plague, wherewith the Lord will smite the heathen that come not up to keep the feast of tabernacles."

—Zech. 14:16–18.

Here we have pictured people, some of whom did not want to go up to Jerusalem "to worship the King, the Lord of hosts, and to keep the feast of tabernacles."

During the personal reign of Christ on earth, there will be people who must be punished and disciplined, even when Satan is chained and shut up in the bottomless pit. We might believe that even Christians, if we were then weak as we now are with our unredeemed bodies, might need such measures to force us to go to worship the Lord Jesus Christ. But we cannot believe that would be necessary with glorified saints. Surely these men who refuse to go to Jerusalem to worship Christ are unconverted, mortal people, people in natural bodies.

But remember also that these are not people deceived by Satan. Christians these days are often deceived by the enemy of our souls. But how could a Christian sin if Satan, the Deceiver, were shut away from us completely and were never allowed to mislead us nor suggest an evil thought or deed? I believe that even Adam and Eve would never have sinned but for Satan's deception and leading. And yet Adam and Eve were not glorified saints in resurrection bodies having been redeemed by the blood of Christ. They were perfect and sinless, having never been lost and so never saved. They were in the image of God, and yet they did not know good and evil before their sin. Surely it is true that with Satan chained in a bottomless pit, those who refuse to obey Christ during the kingdom age will be unsaved people who must be disciplined by drought, according to the verses above.

These same unsaved people will come to active, malicious rebellion when Satan is loosed for a season.

How Will Unsaved Ones Get into the Kingdom of Christ?

That subhead asks a hard question. We know certainly that to all the unsaved accountable men and women of this age, we can safely preach, as Jesus did to Nicodemus, "Except a man be born again, he cannot see the kingdom of God," and "Except a man be born of water and of the Spirit, he cannot enter into the kingdom of God" (John 3:3, 5). Certainly the unsaved people who have rejected Christ as Saviour during all past ages of the world will be shut out of this kingdom of Christ. Of that there can be no doubt. If the sinners without a new birth cannot even see the kingdom of God, much less enter it, then how will it happen that there shall be unsaved people on the earth during the millennial reign of Christ? That is a difficult question, but we must try to find what the Scripture has to say about it and not go beyond what is written.

First, it seems likely that these unsaved people, in natural bodies, will not be born from the Christians in glorified bodies. Remember that the Sadducees came to Jesus with the story of seven men, brothers, who successively had one woman as wife, and asked whose wife she would be in the resurrection. They thought this would prove there was no resurrection. But Jesus answered them, "Ye do err, not knowing the scriptures, nor the power of God. For in the resurrection they neither marry, nor are given in marriage, but are as the angels of God in heaven" (Matt. 22:29, 30). Evidently then in the resurrection saved people will not marry nor have husbands and wives. With no marriage, we have no reason to believe there will be children born from these glorified saints. Any children born during the millennial age would proceed from others in natural bodies.

Who are these unsaved people, in natural bodies, on the earth during the first thousand years of Christ's personal reign? Zechariah 14:16, noticed above, gives us a hint. "And it shall come to pass," that verse tells us, "that every one that is left of all the nations which came against Jerusalem" are to go up to worship the Lord and keep the Feast of Tabernacles; and if they do not keep that appointed feast in Jerusalem annually, they will be punished with drought. Evidently, then, these mentioned are remnants of the nations who will be on the earth in the Great Tribulation time. "Every one that is left of all the nations" must mean that some individuals out of all these nations are gathered over into the kingdom in their natural bodies and there given a chance to trust in Christ and be saved. We would suppose that if they should trust in Christ and be saved, they would be given resurrection bodies. Certainly many Jews will so trust in Christ and be saved after Christ returns in person to Palestine. The Lord has not revealed many details along this line, so let us learn what we can and be content. If it were good for us to know more, the Bible would tell us more.

Some Unsaved Left on Earth After the Judgment of the Living Nations

Zechariah the fourteenth chapter tells how the armies of the nations, under the leadership of the Antichrist, will be gathered against Jerusalem in the day when Christ returns visibly, bodily, to the earth to establish His kingdom. That battle of Armageddon, in the vale of Megiddon outside of Jerusalem, will bring to a close the reign of the Antichrist and so likewise will close the Great Tribulation period and the times of the Gentiles. That will be the end, forever, of the Gentile kingdoms of this earth, and Christ will establish the throne of David, and it shall fill the whole earth.

In Revelation 19:11-21 that return of Christ in glory is pictured and the great battle of Armageddon against "the beast," that is, the Antichrist or world dictator; and we are told how this wicked ruler and his false prophets will be cast alive into Hell, and how the remainder of his army of millions will be put to death and their bodies devoured by the fowls of the air.

But when the army of the Antichrist is disposed of, or the armies of all the nations under the rule of the Antichrist, there yet remains a civilian population of the earth to deal with. Matthew 25:31-46 tells us how Christ will assemble the nations of the earth together before Him for a judgment. That passage is not long, and if you who read it get in mind carefully the setting, that this is a judgment of living people on this earth at the beginning of the reign of Christ, you can understand it and be blessed by it. This is not the last judgment of the unsaved dead, with bodies brought out of the graves and spirits brought out of Hell, for that judgment is at the close of the thousand years as told in Revelation 20:11-15. No, this judgment in Matthew 25 is a thousand years earlier, the judgment of the living Gentiles of the earth, the civilian population left alive after the battle of Armageddon. Christ will sit on the throne of His glory at Jerusalem and pass judgment on them as told in the following verses:

"When the Son of man shall come in his glory, and all the holy angels with him, then shall he sit upon the throne of his glory: And before him shall be gathered all nations: and he shall separate them one from another, as a shepherd divideth his sheep from the goats: And he shall set the sheep on his right hand, but the goats on the left. Then shall the King say unto them on his right hand, Come, ye blessed of my Father, inherit the kingdom prepared for you from the foundation of the world: For I was an hungred, and ye gave me meat: I was thirsty, and ye gave me drink: I was a stranger, and ye took me in: Naked, and ye clothed me: I was sick, and ye visited me: I was in prison, and ye came unto me. Then shall the righteous answer him, saying, Lord, when saw we thee an hungred, and fed thee? or thirsty, and gave thee drink? When saw we thee a stranger, and took thee in? or naked, and clothed thee? Or when saw we thee sick, or in prison, and came unto thee? And the King shall answer and say unto

*them, Verily I say unto you, Inasmuch as ye have done it unto
one of the least of these my brethren, ye have done it unto me.
Then shall he say also unto them on the left hand, Depart from
me, ye cursed, into everlasting fire, prepared for the devil and his
angels: For I was an hungred, and ye gave me no meat: I was
thirsty, and ye gave me no drink: I was a stranger, and ye took me
not in: naked, and ye clothed me not: sick, and in prison, and ye
visited me not. Then shall they also answer him, saying, Lord,
when saw we thee an hungred, or athirst, or a stranger, or naked,
or sick, or in prison, and did not minister unto thee? Then shall
he answer them, saying, Verily I say unto you, Inasmuch as ye
did it not to one of the least of these, ye did it not to me. And
these shall go away into everlasting punishment: but the righteous
into life eternal.*"—Matt. 25:31–46.

Notice there are sheep and goats and brethren present at that
judgment. The brethren are Jews, the blood kin of the Lord
Jesus, who was born of Mary, a Jewess of the tribe of Judah. The
sheep are Gentiles who will befriend the Jews during the Great
Tribulation. The goats are Gentiles who favored the Antichrist.
Now from these Gentile nations in some way there shall be some
left to go into the millennial kingdom, for Zechariah 14:16 refers
to "every one that is left of all the nations which came against
Jerusalem."

Will some of these Gentiles who befriended the Jews and lived
godly lives be unsaved Gentiles who never trusted Christ? I do
not think so. Will little children of these Gentile nations, unac-
countable infants, be carried over into the kingdom in natural
bodies? It seems very likely. Certainly we know that God would
not slay little children and send them to Hell if they were unac-
countable. On the other hand, the Scripture does not expressly
say that such little children will be changed and transformed,
being given glorified bodies. Therefore I believe it likely that
such little children might grow up in the glorious kingdom age
without open rebellion, and yet without a change of heart, and
still in their natural bodies. Such people in natural bodies would
grow to maturity, would marry and have children. Thus it would
not be difficult to account for the multitude as the sand of the
sea which would rebel against Christ at the close of the thousand

years when Satan is loosed out of his prison for a little season to deceive the nations again (Rev. 20:7–9).

Two things are certainly clear. First, unsaved people who reject Christ as Saviour are plainly told that they cannot enter the kingdom of God. If Nicodemus must be born again before he could even see that kingdom, the same is true about all other accountable sinners. There is not the slightest room for any unbeliever to expect that God will take him into the kingdom on earth without a change of heart.

Second, There Will Be Natural Bodies on Earth During the Reign of Christ

Isaiah 11:8 clearly tells us that there will be sucking children on the earth during the millennial reign of Christ. Of whom will these children be born, and whose breasts will they suck? The inference here is that babies will be born and nurse at their mother's breasts during the reign of Christ. But if resurrected people neither marry nor are given in marriage, then these children must be born of unsaved parents, in natural bodies. Isaiah 65:20 must mean no babies will die as so many now do, at just a few days of age, but that natural-born children, during the millennium, will die an hundred years old. But if people die at all during that happy time, they must be people in natural bodies, not the resurrected and glorified saints. Read that verse again and you will see it must be the picture of unsaved people, in natural bodies, on the earth during the millennium. "There shall be no more thence an infant of days, nor an old man that hath not filled his days: for the child shall die an hundred years old; but the sinner being an hundred years old shall be accursed." Under ideal conditions, mankind will fail again. The history of the human race is a story of failure. Adam and Eve, made perfect in a perfect Garden of Eden, listened to the tempter and fell into sin. With them fell in crushing ruin the whole unborn human race.

The Millennium—The Last Probation for the Human Race

Outside the Garden of Eden, God made a new covenant that the seed of the woman should bruise the serpent's head; and I believe Adam and Eve put their faith in that coming Saviour, were forgiven and saved. But the first child ever born, Cain, became a murderer; and from that time forth the whole race degenerated until it repented God that He had made man; and He blotted out all the race but eight souls in a terrible flood.

After the flood God made a covenant with Noah, and Noah, coming out of the ark, built an altar and offered sacrifice to God. But next he planted a vineyard, and next we see him lying drunk and naked. Soon the whole race was building the tower of Babel, and God scattered them to all the earth by the confusion of tongues.

In the midst of idolatry everywhere, God called Abraham and made a new start, with a new race, Israel. But the history of Israel is a history of wickedness and idolatry. They were carried captive to Assyria and Babylon in punishment. When a remnant was brought back to Palestine, and in due time the Saviour came, Israel first rejected and then crucified the Lord of glory. Forty years later God had the city destroyed by the army of Titus, until not one stone of the temple was left upon another; and the long foretold dispersion of Israel to every nation under Heaven took place.

But God had chosen a little handful of Galilean followers, and these started to carry the gospel to all the world. Empowered by the Holy Spirit at Pentecost, they made a marvelous beginning, and there were never days on this earth, I suppose, like those early days of New Testament churches; revivals, power, rejoicing, and spreading of the gospel. But too soon the fires began to cool. The gospel seed became a tree of denominationalism and human organization, and in the tree, the foul birds of wickedness and modernism come to make their nests. In the three measures of meal, a woman hid leaven until the whole was leavened. Paul was inspired to write Timothy that "evil men and seducers shall wax worse and worse" (II Tim. 3:13), and that "in the last days perilous times shall come" (II Tim. 3:1). In Revelation the third chapter, the last period of the church age is pictured as one where God's people are neither cold nor hot and nauseate God by their indifference until He spews them out of His mouth. During the church age, as during all other ages, mankind has failed God.

But in the coming kingdom of Christ on earth, God will set out a thousand years for the last time when mankind will be proved. The Saviour Himself will rule the whole earth. His saints will rule with Him. Even Satan will be chained in the bottomless pit until not a sinner will be deceived as to the facts concerning Christ and righteousness. It will be a new Garden of Eden on the earth. And mankind, that is, unregenerate mankind, mankind after the flesh, will fail again under those conditions as he has under every other condition.

Does not God know that sinful mankind will fail, even under the best of circumstances? Yes, He knows, but He wants all the redeemed to know it, all the doomed in Hell to know it, all the angels to know it, and all the demons to know it throughout the millions of years of eternity!

One thing must stand out in every dealing of God with man, and that is this: *salvation is wholly of Christ!* Man never did, and man never will, earn the favor of God. God seems determined to prove to every created being His great mercy toward mankind.

A review of these facts ought to help you to see the truth of Ephesians 2:4–9, which says:

"But God, who is rich in mercy, for his great love wherewith he loved us, Even when we were dead in sins, hath quickened us together with Christ, (by grace ye are saved;) And hath raised us up together, and made us sit together in heavenly places in Christ Jesus: That in the ages to come he might shew the exceeding riches of his grace in his kindness toward us through Christ Jesus. For by grace are ye saved through faith; and that not of yourselves: it is the gift of God: Not of works, lest any man should boast."

Knowing that God wishes to show His mercy and to be publicly justified in the sight of all creation in His dealing with men, we can understand how He will allow unsaved people to be tested on the earth during the millennial reign of Christ.

Chapter 13

What Must Come Before the Kingdom—Looking for Jesus

THE BIBLE, the Book of all books, gives so much space to prophecies of the future that it is impossible to discuss them all in this volume. This book is about the coming kingdom of Christ, not about the rapture of the saints, the tribulation period, the reign of the Antichrist nor the Battle of Armageddon. So we will not discuss those events in much detail. This chapter will only seek to give a brief outline of the events that must come before the kingdom of Christ begins on earth.

It is very important to know that the reign of Christ is not the next or first event on God's program. Casual, unspiritual or unbelieving readers of the Bible have sometimes said that there were contradictory Scriptures concerning the second coming of Christ; that some Scriptures appeared to teach that Jesus might come at any moment, while other verses appeared to teach that other things must intervene before the coming of Christ. Such readers were confused by not distinguishing between the different phases of Christ's coming. Truly, we are commanded, "Watch therefore, for ye know neither the day nor the hour wherein the Son of man cometh" (Matt. 25:13). But that Scripture refers to Christ's coming into the air to take away His saints, the event often called the rapture. Such Scriptures do not refer to Christ's physical appearance on this earth with saints and angels to take over the reins of world government in a literal kingdom.

In Bible times, some Christians were confused about this very matter. At Thessalonica, some had been taught to expect "the day of Christ" or "the day of the Lord," that is, the day of Christ's enthronement and reign, to begin at any time. This is made apparent in II Thessalonians 2:1–12.

> "*Now we beseech you, brethren, by the coming of our Lord Jesus Christ, and by our gathering together unto him, 2 That ye be not soon shaken in mind, or be troubled, neither by spirit, nor by word, nor by letter as from us, as that the day of Christ is at hand. 3 Let no man deceive you by any means: for that day shall not come, except there come a falling away first, and that man of sin be revealed, the son of perdition; 4 Who opposeth and exalteth himself above all that is called God, or that is worshipped; so that he as God sitteth in the temple of God, shewing himself that he is God. 5 Remember ye not, that, when I was yet with you, I told you these things? 6 And now ye know what withholdeth that he might be revealed in his time. 7 For the mystery of iniquity doth already work: only he who now letteth will let, until he be taken out of the way. 8 And then shall that Wicked be revealed, whom the Lord shall consume with the spirit of his mouth, and shall destroy with the brightness of his coming: 9 Even him, whose coming is after the working of Satan with all power and signs and lying wonders, 10 And with all deceivableness of unrighteousness in them that perish; because they received not the love of the truth, that they might be saved. 11 And for this cause God shall send them strong delusion, that they should believe a lie: 12 That they all might be damned who believed not the truth, but had pleasure in unrighteousness.*"

From the above Scripture, it is evident that the day of Christ, that is, the period of His vengeance and reign, is not to be expected immediately. First, the Scripture says that there must come a falling away and the Man of Sin be revealed. According to verse 8, this Man of Sin will reign until the day of Christ when he will be destroyed by the brightness of Christ's coming.

Suppose we check by this Scripture certain things that must come before the reign of Christ on earth.

1. A great "falling away" (v. 3).
2. The One who now hinders or lets will be taken out of the way before the Man of Sin is revealed (vs. 6, 7).
3. The Man of Sin will sit in the temple showing himself that

he is God (v. 4). (This is evidently the abomination of desolation mentioned in Daniel 9:27 and Matthew 24:15).

4. Multitudes will be deceived by this Man of Sin, or Antichrist, being turned over to a reprobate mind to believe lies (vs. 10–12).

5. The Man of Sin will be destroyed with the brightness of His coming (verse 8).

The above passage clearly shows that all five of these matters must occur before the reign of Christ on earth. We must not expect the reign of Christ on earth to begin at once. Some other things must come first.

The Great Falling Away—Sin and Worldliness Among Christians

Second Thessalonians 2:3 says, "That day shall not come, except there come a falling away first." I believe that this refers to the rapture of the saints, when the invisible ties of gravity will be broken and we will suddenly fall away into the air to meet Jesus. Many believe that this refers to a falling away from sound doctrine, from godly living, from soul-winning devotion. Certainly there is that kind of apostasy. There is modernism and worldliness.

But I remind you that before New Testament days had passed, this falling away had set in. Paul began the gospel work at Corinth, and yet a little later found it necessary to write back to his converts, rebuking them for all kinds of sin and worldliness: division, strife, drunkenness, adultery, going to law with Christians, and disorders in the church services. His Galatian converts turned back to legalism and were misled by the Judaisers, thinking circumcision necessary to salvation. New Testament churches of which we are given continued record all came to their time of falling away.

A clear example is the case of the church at Ephesus, perhaps the most spiritual of all New Testament churches. There Paul spent three years. But Christ, in Revelation 2:4 sent the message to this church at Ephesus, "I have somewhat against thee, because thou hast left thy first love."

The church at Rome whose faith was spoken of throughout the whole world (Romans 1:8) became the mother of the papacy.

The falling away which was to come before the reign of Christ is not new to the present age. It has been in progress ever since the ascension of Christ. It has only gotten worse as the centuries have gone by.

The Rapture of the Saints—the Next Thing on God's Program

The first fulfillment of prophecy that we should expect, the next thing on God's program as revealed in the Bible, is Christ's coming into the air to receive His saints and to take them away for a honeymoon in Heaven. The falling away is a progressive matter. On that, the Scripture is already fulfilled. But repeatedly, in the gospels and in the letters of Paul, we are commanded to expect the coming of Christ at any moment. Notice the following warnings from the mouth of Jesus:

"Watch therefore: for ye know not what hour your Lord doth come."—Matt. 24:42.

"Therefore be ye also ready: for in such an hour as ye think not the Son of man cometh."—Matt. 24:44.

"Watch therefore, for ye know neither the day nor the hour wherein the Son of man cometh."—Matt. 25:13.

"But of that day and that hour knoweth no man, no, not the angels which are in heaven, neither the Son, but the Father. Take ye heed, watch and pray: for ye know not when the time is. For the Son of man is as a man taking a far journey, who left his house, and gave authority to his servants, and to every man his work, and commanded the porter to watch. Watch ye therefore: for ye know not when the master of the house cometh, at even, or at midnight, or at the cockcrowing, or in the morning: Lest coming suddenly he find you sleeping. And what I say unto you I say unto all, Watch."—Mark 13:32–37.

"Watch ye therefore, and pray always, that ye may be accounted worthy to escape all these things that shall come to pass, and to stand before the Son of man."—Luke 21:36.

Jesus told even His own disciples to watch for His return. If the Scripture may be taken at face value, and if Jesus meant what He said, then His return was an event for which no date was set, one that might occur at any moment. In other words, the return of Christ for His saints is imminent. By this term we mean that at any time since the ascension, Jesus might have returned, and it has been the duty of every Christian to watch for the coming and expect His coming every moment since that time. No one knows the time when Jesus will return, but every Christian should be ready at any moment.

Paul expected to be alive when Jesus returns for His saints. First Thessalonians 4:15–18 says:

"For this we say unto you by the word of the Lord, that we which are alive and remain unto the coming of the Lord shall not prevent them which are asleep. For the Lord himself shall descend from heaven with a shout, with the voice of the archangel, and with the trump of God: and the dead in Christ shall rise first: Then we which are alive and remain shall be caught up together with them in the clouds, to meet the Lord in the air: and so shall we ever be with the Lord. Wherefore comfort one another with these words."

Paul said, "WE which are alive and remain shall be caught up. . . ." Paul expected to be alive and remaining on the earth when Jesus comes. In this he was obeying the plain command of Christ to watch. Only shortly before his death was it revealed to him so that he could say, "The time of my departure is at hand."

The coming of Christ for His saints and their rapturous ascent with Him to Heaven is referred to in I Corinthians 15:51, 52 as follows:

"Behold, I shew you a mystery; We shall not all sleep, but we shall all be changed, In a moment, in the twinkling of an eye, at the last trump: for the trumpet shall sound, and the dead shall be raised incorruptible, and we shall be changed."

From the above Scriptures several things are clear about the rapture.

1. It will come very suddenly, Jesus said, as a thief in the night (Matt. 24:43; I Thess. 5:2), in a day and hour when people are not expecting it.

2. It will be marked with a shout, with the voice of the archangel and with the trump of God.

3. Instantly, "in the twinkling of an eye," the bodies of the

Christian dead will be resurrected, glorified, caught up in the air to meet Christ.

4. The living saints will likewise be changed "In the twinkling of an eye" and caught up with those who are resurrected out of the graves. Both groups together will meet Christ in the air and go with Him to the place which He has prepared for us in the Father's house of many mansions. Jesus said in John 14:3, "And if I go and prepare a place for you, I will come again, and receive you unto myself, that where I am, there ye may be also."

This is the great event for which Christians should constantly watch and be ready. Jesus is coming! He comes not to reign on the earth as yet, but He may come today to take away His bride. "Watch therefore, for ye know neither the day nor the hour wherein the Son of man cometh" (Matt. 25:13).

"The Man of Sin" Must Be Revealed

Second Thessalonians 2:8 says that the Man of Sin must be revealed before the day and reign of Christ on earth.

The Man of Sin is known by several terms in the Bible. He is called "the Man of Sin," "the son of perdition." He is pictured by the "little horn" in the head of the beast in Daniel chapter 7. He is "the prince that shall come" of Daniel 9:26. In Revelation 13, he has become not just one of the horns, but the whole "beast," the absolute ruler of the restored Roman Empire. He will be the incarnation of Satan's power, for we are told, "The dragon gave him his power, and his seat, and great authority" (Rev. 13:2). We are told that this terrible figure, this man of whom Pharaoh and Judas Iscariot were types, must be revealed before the Lord Jesus comes to reign, and then he will be destroyed by the brightness of Christ's coming.

This Man of Sin is not yet revealed, and he cannot be named. However, so many details are given about his character, location, people, rise and rule that the study is of fascinating interest. Notice the following facts:

1. This ruler or dictator will arise among the ten kingdoms which are the fragments remaining after the dissolution of the Roman Empire (Daniel 7:19–24). He rises among the ten horns, out of the beast that was Rome.

Again, he himself will be a Roman, of the same people as the army of Titus which destroyed Jerusalem in A.D. 70 (for he is the prince mentioned in Daniel 9:26, a prince of the people that destroyed the sanctuary).

He will make a treaty with the Jews, allowing them to return to Jerusalem, rebuild their temple, and begin anew their Old Testament sacrifices (Dan. 9:27). The covenant will be for one seven of years (translated week). This week must be a week of seven literal years, as a study of Daniel 9:24–27 plainly shows. Seventy weeks of national history were assigned to Daniel's people Israel, in their land, Canaan. Sixty-nine of those weeks, or 483 years, were to last from the time that the command went forth to restore Jerusalem in the days of Ezra and Nehemiah down to the first coming of Christ. Those sixty-nine weeks have already occurred and each week was seven years as prophesied. Then when Jesus came, and was rejected, the veil of the temple was torn down, Jews were soon scattered to all parts of the world, and God called "time out" for the Jews until the last week begins. The last week will be this week of seven years when many Jews will be brought back again to Jerusalem and will start their sacrifices in their temple at Jerusalem. That week, then, like the sixty-nine others which have already occurred, must be seven years; and half of it will be three and one-half years or forty-two months, or 1,260 days. The Antichrist will make a treaty with the Jews, allowing them to return to Palestine and restore their temple and worship for a literal period of seven years. This indicates that the Man of Sin will have a mandate or a political control over Palestine.

Since this treaty or covenant with the Jews is the first clearly taught and unmistakable public act of the Man of Sin, it appears likely that by this treaty he will be revealed to the world as the Man of Sin. Any man who arises as a dictator in Italy, gains control over Palestine and makes a treaty with the Jews of the world, allowing them to rebuild their temple and begin their Old Testament sacrifices, that man will obviously be known by the Scripture as the Man of Sin or Antichrist.

Afterwards, in the middle of the seven years of the covenant with the Jews, the Man of Sin will enter into the temple at Jerusalem and commit the abomination of desolation, causing the sacrifices and oblation to cease, "showing himself that he is God."

Read II Thessalonians 2:3, 4 with Daniel 9:27. This must happen three and one half years, or half the week, after the Man of Sin is made known.

The last half of the week of seven years, the Man of Sin will reign with an absolute distatorship over the whole world, "over all kindreds, and tongues, and nations" (Rev. 13:7). Then his terrible world-wide reign will continue three and one-half years. This is the "time and times and the dividing of time" of Daniel 7:25 and the "time, and times, and half a time" of Revelation 12:14. It is the forty-two months of Revelation 11:2 and of Revelation 13:5. It is the 1,260 days of Revelation 11:3 and Revelation 12:6. These three and one-half years are often called "the Great Tribulation" from Matthew 24:21 and Revelation 7:14.

During this time of great tribulation, the Jews will be in rebellion against the Man of Sin and will be terribly persecuted, and many will be put to death. The woman who brings forth a man child in Revelation, chapter 12, is evidently Israel, from whom Christ came according to the flesh. When she flees away into the wilderness for 1,260 days (Rev. 12:6) that will evidently be this great time of tribulation. It is called in Jeremiah 30:7 "the time of Jacob's trouble."

Man of Sin Cannot Be Revealed Until After Jesus Comes for His Saints

As we have said before, the next thing on God's program is the sound of the trumpet and the voice of the archangel that will call the bodies of sleeping saints in glorified form from their graves and will change the living saints in a moment, in the twinkling of an eye, and catch us all away to meet Jesus in the air. Many Scriptures warn us to be ready for the coming of the Saviour. Clearly then, the rapture of the saints must take place before the Man of Sin is revealed.

This is taught in II Thessalonians 2:7, 8 which we have studied above. Those verses say:

"For the mystery of iniquity doth already work: only he who now letteth will let, until he be taken out of the way. And then shall that Wicked be revealed, whom the Lord shall consume with the spirit of his mouth, and shall destroy with the brightness of his coming."

There is One, a powerful Person who hinders the appearance of the Antichrist or Man of Sin. The Man of Sin cannot be revealed until this One is taken out of the way. Who is He? He has been in the world these 1,900 years; so it cannot be any living man. This does not refer to Christ, because Christ with His physical body was taken away and ascended to Heaven where He now sits at the right hand of the Father. It was not even the church, since the Scripture never refers to the church as "he." This One who hinders the Man of Sin must be the Holy Spirit. At the rapture of the saints, we believe, the Holy Spirit will be taken out of the way of the Man of Sin so that he may be revealed.

I do not mean that the Holy Spirit will not work any more in this world. The Spirit of God is everywhere on the earth and always has been. The Scripture shows that some will be saved during the tribulation time (Rev. 7:1–14; Rev. 20:4). The two witnesses will prophesy in the power of the Spirit during the tribulation time (Rev. 11:1–12). The Holy Spirit will not be out of this world after the rapture. But certain it is, that when the bodies of all the saved people in the earth are caught up to meet Christ in the air, in that sense, the human temples of the Holy Spirit will be taken away, and His influence through these will be gone. That is, the influence of the Holy Spirit on the world through the lives and testimonies of born-again people will be removed and the Man of Sin will then be revealed, the Scripture teaches.

Those of us who live now, having trusted in Christ for salvation, will not see the Man of Sin nor suffer under His rule of Satanic power and wickedness. We will be with Christ at the wedding supper, prepared by the Father for His dear Son and for us, the Son's bride. The Man of Sin cannot be revealed until after the rapture of the saints.

The Plagues of the Great Tribulation

The reign of the Man of Sin will be such a time of tribulation as was never in this world before "no, nor ever shall be" (Matt. 24:21). We can only suggest some of the sorrows of that time.

A comparison of the book of Revelation with Exodus will show that the plagues in Egypt were only types which faintly foreshadowed the more terrible plagues that will be on this earth. Pharaoh was a type of the Antichrist, the Man of Sin, as Moses was the type of our Lord Jesus Christ. Egypt was a type of the world. As in Egypt water was turned to blood, so it will be during the tribulation period. The locusts in Egypt were types of the "locusts" in Revelation 9, really demons from Hell who will enter into the followers of the Man of Sin and his army. The plague of frogs in Egypt pictured the frogs which are the spirits of devils, which during the great tribulation will deceive the kings of the East and lead them to their utter destruction in the Battle of Armageddon (Revelation 16:13, 14). And the death of the first-born in Egypt was only a taste of what will occur in the Great Tribulation. First, one fourth of the population and then one third of the remainder will die of war, famine and pestilence (Rev. 6:8; Rev. 9:15). Later, the entire army of the Man of Sin, two hundred million soldiers (Rev. 9:16) will be slain in a day at the Battle of Armageddon (Rev. 19:11–21). Their blood will make a river two hundred miles long and as deep as the bridles of the horses (Rev. 14:20) and the beasts of the earth will devour the flesh of men and captains and bondmen and freemen as well as their horses. Then the Lord Jesus will smite the Man of Sin with the brightness of His coming, and he with his false prophet will be cast into the lake of fire.

The Glorious Return of Christ to Reign

The most awful and terrifying event this world will ever see will be the literal, personal, bodily return of Christ to reign. Of this return, the two angels who stood by in white apparel said to the apostles after the ascent of Jesus: "Ye men of Galilee, why stand ye gazing up into heaven? this same Jesus, which is taken up from you into heaven, shall so come in like manner as ye have seen him go into heaven" (Acts 1:11).

Jesus was caught up into Heaven until the clouds received Him out of their sight (Acts 1:9). He will return in clouds, for Revelation 1:7 says: "Behold, he cometh with clouds; and every eye shall see him, and they also which pierced him: and all kindreds of the earth shall wail because of him. Even so, Amen."

Matthew 24:29–31 tells us likewise that Jesus will come with clouds:

"Immediately after the tribulation of those days shall the sun be darkened, and the moon shall not give her light, and the stars

shall fall from heaven, and the powers of the heavens shall be shaken: And then shall appear the sign of the Son of man in heaven: and then shall all the tribes of the earth mourn, and they shall see the Son of man coming in the clouds of heaven with power and great glory. And he shall send his angels with a great sound of a trumpet, and they shall gather together his elect from the four winds, from one end of heaven to the other."

Jesus ascended to Heaven from the Mount of Olives or Olivet, and Zechariah 14:4 says, "His feet shall stand in that day upon the mount of Olives, which is before Jerusalem on the east."

Jesus went away with a physical body, a body that ate and drank, a body with hands and feet, a body of flesh and bones; and He will return the same way.

The glorious return of Christ! No wonder "all nations shall mourn because of Him!" That is, the people on earth who do not love and serve Him will be seized in an agony of apprehension when they see the Lord Jesus! For He comes this time not the suffering Servant, not the meek and lowly Saviour, not the gentle "Lamb of God that taketh the sin of the world." No, when Jesus returns in clouds to reign, He will come as "the Lion of the tribe of Judah," to trample under feet His enemies, to shed their blood in vengeance instead of His own in atonement. Christ will come the second time, to the Jews, as the Sun of righteousness with healing in His wings and will open up to the house of David a fountain for sin and uncleanness, because at that time the whole nation of Israel, then alive, will turn and seek Him and love Him, and with penitent hearts will receive Him. But to the nations as a whole, living in wickedness and violence under the rule of the Man of Sin, Christ will come as a terrible Judge.

Let us allow the words from the Book of God to tell us again of this coming of Christ.

"And I saw heaven opened, and behold a white horse; and he that sat upon him was called Faithful and True, and in righteousness he doth judge and make war. His eyes were as a flame of fire, and on his head were many crowns; and he had a name written, that no man knew, but he himself. And he was clothed with a vesture dipped in blood: and his name is called The Word of God. And the armies which were in heaven followed him upon

*white horses, clothed in fine linen, white and clean. And out of
his mouth goeth a sharp sword, that with it he should smite the
nations; and he shall rule them with a rod of iron: and he
treadeth the winepress of the fierceness and wrath of Almighty
God. And he hath on his vesture and on his thigh a name written,
KING OF KINGS, AND LORD OF LORDS. And I saw an
angel standing in the sun; and he cried with a loud voice, saying
to all the fowls that fly in the midst of heaven, Come and gather
yourselves together unto the supper of the great God; That ye
may eat the flesh of kings, and the flesh of captains, and the
flesh of mighty men, and the flesh of horses, and of them that sit
on them, and the flesh of all men, both free and bond, both
small and great. And I saw the beast, and the kings of the earth,
and their armies, gathered together to make war against him that
sat on the horse, and against his army. And the beast was taken,
and with him the false prophet that wrought miracles before
him, with which he deceived them that had received the mark
of the beast, and them that worshipped his image. These both
were cast alive into a lake of fire burning with brimstone. And
the remnant were slain with the sword of him that sat upon the
horse, which sword proceeded out of his mouth: and all the fowls
were filled with their flesh.*"—Rev. 19:11–21.

"*Behold, the day of the Lord cometh, and thy spoil shall be
divided in the midst of thee. For I will gather all nations against
Jerusalem to battle; and the city shall be taken, and the houses
rifled, and the women ravished; and half of the city shall go
forth into captivity, and the residue of the people shall not be cut
off from the city. Then shall the Lord go forth, and fight against
those nations, as when he fought in the day of battle. And his feet
shall stand in that day upon the mount of Olives, which is before
Jerusalem on the east, and the mount of Olives shall cleave in the
midst thereof toward the east and toward the west, and there shall
be a very great valley; and half of the mountain shall remove
toward the north, and half of it toward the south. And ye shall
flee to the valley of the mountains; for the valley of the mountains
shall reach unto Azal: yea, ye shall flee, like as ye fled from before
the earthquake in the days of Uzziah king of Judah: and the Lord
my God shall come, and all the saints with thee. And it shall come
to pass in that day, that the light shall not be clear, nor dark:*

But it shall be one day which shall be known to the Lord, not day, nor night: but it shall come to pass, that at evening time it shall be light. And it shall be in that day, that living waters shall go out from Jerusalem; half of them toward the former sea, and half of them toward the hinder sea: in summer and in winter shall it be. And the Lord shall be king over all the earth: in that day shall there be one Lord, and his name one."—Zech. 14:1–9.

The Judgment of the Living Nations

No one part of the Bible tells the whole story. In the gospel of Matthew, the Lord tells of another great event that follows the Battle of Armageddon after the soldiers in the armies of the Man of Sin are all put to death in one day. Then Christ will sit on the throne of His glory and judge the civilian population which remains alive on the earth. Matthew 25:31–46 tells the story as follows:

"When the Son of man shall come in his glory, and all the holy angels with him, then shall he sit upon the throne of his glory: And before him shall be gathered all nations: and he shall separate them one from another, as a shepherd divideth his sheep from the goats: And he shall set the sheep on his right hand, but the goats on the left. Then shall the King say unto them on his right hand, Come, ye blessed of my Father, inherit the kingdom prepared for you from the foundation of the world: For I was an hungred, and ye gave me meat: I was thirsty, and ye gave me drink: I was a stranger, and ye took me in: Naked, and ye clothed me: I was sick, and ye visited me: I was in prison, and ye came unto me. Then shall the righteous answer him, saying, Lord, when saw we thee an hungred, and fed thee? or thirsty, and gave thee drink? When saw we thee a stranger, and took thee in? or naked, and clothed thee? Or when saw we thee sick, or in prison, and came unto thee? And the King shall answer and say unto them, Verily I say unto you, Inasmuch as ye have done it unto one of the least of these my brethren, ye have done it unto me. Then shall he say also unto them on the left hand, Depart from me, ye cursed, into everlasting fire, prepared for the devil and his angels: For I was an hungred, and ye gave me no meat: I was

thirsty, and ye gave me no drink: I was a stranger, and ye took me not in: naked, and ye clothed me not: sick, and in prison, and ye visited me not. Then shall they also answer him, saying, Lord, when saw we thee an hungred, or athirst, or a stranger, or naked, or sick, or in prison, and did not minister unto thee? Then shall he answer them, saying, Verily I say unto you, Inasmuch as ye did it not to one of the least of these, ye did it not to me. And these shall go away into everlasting punishment: but the righteous into life eternal."

Notice who are those judged: before Him shall be gathered all nations (v. 32). THIS IS NOT A JUDGMENT OF THE DEAD. It has often been misunderstood and confused with the great white throne judgment in Revelation 20:11–15. The two judgments are not the same. This is on earth. That in Revelation 20 is out in space. This one is at the beginning of the thousand years reign, that in Revelation chapter 20 is at the end of the thousand years reign. This in Matthew 25 is a judgment of the LIVING nations, but in Revelation 20, John says, "I saw the DEAD, small and great, stand before God." The two are not the same. Here the dead do not appear. This is a judgment of the civilian population of the earth at the close of the Battle of Armageddon and after Christ first sits upon the throne of His glory.

Those mentioned as present in this judgment are three classes, sheep, goats, and brethren. The "sheep" are Gentile Christians, converted during the tribulation time. The proof that they love God is that they will have sided against the Man of Sin who will claim to be God on earth and taken sides for the Jews who will still believe in the God of Heaven and refuse to worship the Antichrist. The "goats" are unsaved Gentiles. The "brethren" are Israelites, Jews, the brethren of Jesus Christ according to the flesh.

Notice that the saved Gentiles will hear the words of Christ, "Come, ye blessed of my Father, inherit the kingdom prepared for you from the foundation of the world" (verse 34). The unsaved Gentiles who were left alive after the Battle of Armageddon will receive the condemnation: "Depart from me, ye cursed, into everlasting fire, prepared for the devil and his angels." The Jews will be assembled from all the world back to Palestine and there will be converted. The unsaved Gentiles will be sent to Hell, and the saved Gentiles will enter into the kingdom with Christ and the Jews and with all the redeemed who have returned with Christ from the wedding in Heaven.

The millennial reign of Christ then will be well begun.

Chapter 14

No Signs of Christ's Coming

TWICE this book has been reset in type and each time this chapter on signs of Christ's coming has been revised. Each time I needed to modify further the teaching. Now for a fourth edition, after months of prayer and study, I am led to rewrite the chapter entirely. I find it did not heretofore emphasize, as much as it ought, the one great central teaching of Christ and the apostles, that Jesus Christ may come at any moment, that His coming is imminent.

Christ's coming is imminent. That means that Jesus may come at any moment. That means that there is no other prophesied event which must occur before Christ's coming. Nothing else needs to happen before Jesus may come. No signs need precede it. Jesus may come today. He could have come at any time since Pentecost. It is a glad event hanging over us for which we should expectantly await. The coming of Christ is imminent.

I do not mean that "Jesus is coming soon," as so many people say. He may come soon; He may not come for five hundred years. I do not know, no one knows. But His coming is possible at any moment and we should expect it.

I do not mean that certain signs have appeared which indicate that Christ is coming soon. We do not need signs; we simply need to believe and heed His plain statements in the Bible. He commanded us to watch, and we should watch, knowing that He may come at any time.

I do not mean that there is any special evidence that we are "in the end of the age" or that these are "the closing days," as so many people say. I believe that is wrong and unscriptural. I do not believe that anybody in the world knows how close to the end we are. When I say that the coming of Jesus Christ is imminent, I do not mean that there is any special evidence that anybody can give that this age is drawing to an end. I simply mean that He may come at any moment, as He said He might, and we should watch for His coming.

I do not mean that we should expect Christ's coming because of world events. No, we should expect His coming because He said for us to expect Him. We should expect His coming not by sight but by faith, not by the newspapers, but by the Word of God. At any moment, day or night, Jesus may come to call all the redeemed up in the air to meet Him, with those that sleep in Christ raised from the dead, and with us who are alive and remain changed in a moment and caught up together with them to meet the Lord in the air.

This is the one most important phase of the doctrine of Christ's Second Coming. It is the one part of that doctrine which is most emphasized in the New Testament. To get this matter straight and clear in our minds will keep us from many heresies and mistakes and from many a false emphasis.

We Are Commanded to Watch Always for Christ's Imminent Coming

That Christ's Second Coming is imminent, that every Christian should watch continually for it, is made clear by the commands of the Lord Jesus. Also the teachings of the apostles are that Christians are to watch, to wait, to look for Jesus.

1. Note How Definite Are the Commands of Jesus to Watch for His Coming

In Matthew 24:42 Jesus said, "Watch therefore: for ye know not what hour your Lord doth come."

The *therefore* refers to what Jesus has just said above, that the coming of the Son of man will be as sudden and unexpected as the coming of the flood in the days of Noah. He said that of two in a field, one shall be taken and the other left; of two grinding at the mill, the one shall be taken and the other left; and therefore, because of the unexpected suddenness of Christ's coming, we should watch.

Again read the command of Jesus repeated in the next verses:

"But know this, that if the goodman of the house had known in what watch the thief would come, he would have watched and would not have suffered his house to be broken up. Therefore be ye also ready: for in such an hour as ye think not the Son of man cometh."—Matt. 24:43, 44.

Here the Saviour's return for His saints is said to be as sudden and as unexpected as the coming of a thief in the night. Therefore a Christian is to be ready, always ready, "for in such an hour as ye think not the Son of man cometh." Then the following verses tell how blessed is the servant who watches for his master and how displeased his master will be with the servant that does not look for his master and is not ready when he returns.

In Matthew 25 we have the story of the ten virgins and of the midnight cry, "Behold, the bridegroom cometh; go ye out to meet him." And we are told of five foolish virgins who had no oil and were left outside the wedding. Then Jesus gives the application, "Watch therefore, for ye know neither the day nor the hour wherein the Son of man cometh" (Matt. 25:13).

The same command to watch is repeated again and again in the words of Jesus. In Mark He says:

"Take ye heed, watch and pray: for ye know not when the time is. For the Son of man is as a man taking a far journey, who left his house, and gave authority to his servants, and to every man his work, and commanded the porter to watch. Watch ye therefore: for ye know not when the master of the house cometh, at even, or at midnight, or at the cockcrowing, or in the morning: Lest coming suddenly he find you sleeping. And what I say unto you I say unto all, Watch."—Mark 13:33-37.

How solemn, how urgent is the command! Verse 33 says, "Take ye heed, watch and pray: for ye know not when the time is." Verse 35 says, "Watch ye therefore." Verse 37 says, "And what I say unto you I say unto all, Watch." Now it is quite clear that if any one of the disciples watched daily for Jesus after He went away, and thought He might return at any moment, he was only taking at face value the solemn words of the Saviour. And we must say that if at any time since

Jesus went away a Christian, reading these words, expected his Lord's return and solemnly prepared each day to greet the Master, or each night thought that his sleep might be interrupted with the glad trumpet sound and the voice of the archangel, he could not be accused of unfaithfulness. He did exactly what Jesus said a Christian was to do. And today we are commanded to watch and expect Jesus' coming at any time. These Scriptures certainly teach that the coming of Jesus Christ may occur at any moment and that all of us ought to be ready and waiting for that event.

2. Other Scriptures Likewise Command Us to Look for Christ's Coming at Any Moment

All through the rest of the New Testament, if one reads observantly, he will find this attitude of expectancy is taught, just as in the gospels.

Read with me these inspired words written to the Philippians:

"For our conversation is in heaven; from whence also we look for the Saviour, the Lord Jesus Christ: Who shall change our vile body, that it may be fashioned like unto his glorious body, according to the working whereby he is able even to subdue all things unto himself."—Phil. 3:20, 21.

Here the word *conversation* means citizenship. Our citizenship is in Heaven. We are to have our minds on Heaven, not on this world, because from Heaven is coming the Saviour for us. ". . . . whence also we look for the Saviour, the Lord Jesus Christ . . ." Every New Testament Christian was taught to look for the Saviour's coming. We today have the same command.

When Paul began his work among the Thessalonians, many of them were saved. And when they were saved Paul taught them that they were to wait for Christ's coming. He says:

"For they themselves shew of us what manner of entering in we had unto you, and how ye turned to God from idols to serve the living and true God; And to wait for his Son from heaven, whom he raised from the dead, even Jesus, which delivered us from the wrath to come."—I Thess. 1:9, 10.

When the people of Thessalonica turned to God, they turned "to wait for his Son from heaven." To these Christians the second coming of Christ in the future was as glorious and real as His first coming to redeem them. This expectant attitude, taught by the Spirit of God through Paul, means that the coming of Christ must be imminent; that is that Jesus may come at any moment. He could have come then or He could have come at any time since then. Likewise, He may come today.

In I Thessalonians 4:13–18 Paul gives an inspired account of the coming of Christ, when those who are asleep in Christ will not be left behind but Jesus will come from Heaven with a shout:

". . . and the dead in Christ shall rise first: Then we which are alive and remain shall be caught up together with them in the clouds, to meet the Lord in the air: and so shall we ever be with the Lord. Wherefore comfort one another with these words."

Note that here the Thessalonians were to comfort one another with glad expectancy of meeting their loved ones at Christ's Second Coming. They were not taught to look forward to death, but to look forward to Christ's coming. That means that Jesus could have come at any moment, even during their lifetime, and may come now at any moment.

In I Timothy 6:14 Paul was inspired to command Timothy, "That thou keep this commandment without spot, unrebukable, until the appearing of our Lord Jesus Christ." Timothy was to expect Christ's coming in his lifetime.

Paul taught young preachers that they must teach the imminent coming of Christ. In Titus 2:11–13 we read:

"For the grace of God that bringeth salvation hath appeared to all men, Teaching us that, denying ungodliness and worldly lusts, we should live soberly, righteously, and godly, in this present world; Looking for that blessed hope, and the glorious appearing of the great God and our Saviour Jesus Christ."

Here we see that it was an integral part of the gospel message that Christians should continually be "looking for that blessed hope, and the glorious appearing of the great God and our

Saviour Jesus Christ." Titus was to teach people to look for Christ's coming. So it was proper for them to expect that Jesus might come at any moment. Christ was to be expected before there was any World War I or World War II, before any of the so-called present-day signs of Christ's coming could appear. The second coming of Jesus Christ is to be expected continually, without any other basis except that He plainly promised He would return and that He commanded us to watch.

What should be the attitude of a Christian in this present world? He should be "looking for that blessed hope, and the glorious appearing of the great God and our Saviour Jesus Christ."

Now the clear teaching of Christ and of the inspired writers is that every Christian should be watching, should be looking for, should be waiting for Christ's coming. An honest God who puts those things in His Bible must mean that His Son may come at any moment. There is no other honest and fair meaning to be drawn from these plain words. Every Christian should watch daily, hourly, for Christ's return.

3. Paul Himself Continually Expected Christ to Come During His Lifetime

It seems that, just before Paul was beheaded at Rome, God revealed to him that he would die. And he wrote Timothy, "For I am now ready to be offered, and the time of my departure is at hand" (II Tim. 4:6). But before that, in his epistles, Paul had, by divine inspiration, expressed the glad hope that he himself would be alive and remaining to meet Christ at His Second Coming.

For example, see what Paul says in I Corinthians 15:52, "In a moment, in the twinkling of an eye, at the last trump: for the trumpet shall sound, and the dead shall be raised incorruptible, and *we* shall be changed."

Here Paul says that two groups will be wonderfully transformed when Christ comes. The Christian dead, those asleep in Jesus, will be raised from the dead. The Christians left still alive on the earth will be changed in a moment. And with which group did Paul expect to be numbered? He expected to be with those still living! "For the trumpet shall sound, and the dead shall be raised incorruptible, and WE shall be changed," he says. God put in Paul's heart the glad expectation that he would be alive when Jesus came.

The same thing is clear in the way Paul wrote the Thessalonians. He said, "And the dead in Christ shall rise first: Then *we* which are alive and remain shall be caught up together with them in the clouds, to meet the Lord in the air . . ." (I Thess. 4:16, 17). Here Paul clearly counts himself as likely to be with those still alive when Jesus should come.

Now mark very carefully what Paul said. He did not say that it was revealed to him that he would be alive when Jesus returns. He disclaims any knowledge of when Jesus would return. But God had Paul put down in Holy Writ his glad expectation.

Was Paul wrong? No, he was right! He was looking for Jesus to come. He did not claim to know, but in the language used it becomes clear that he hoped that Christ would come in his lifetime. He was simply looking for the Saviour, waiting for the Saviour, watching for the Saviour, exactly as Christians had been commanded to do, and as we today are likewise commanded to do.

Certainly it becomes clear from the Scriptures we have used that the imminent coming of Christ is a New Testament doctrine. The coming of Christ was gladly expected in New Testament times. And if we, like they, obey the Saviour, we too will be looking for Jesus to come at any moment.

We should remember, too, that New Testament Christians were never exhorted to look for Jesus because of certain signs or historical events. They were simply commanded to watch, and they were to do that by faith, because it was commanded.

In view of this solemn, oft-repeated command to watch for Christ's coming, we know that Jesus could have returned to earth any time after Pentecost. There was no event foretold, after Pentecost, which must precede Christ's coming.

So Christians are not to wait for any signs. Christ could come before any wars, any growth in wickedness, before any origin of a new nation Israel. World events are not to influence the Christian in this matter. We are simply to watch for Christ to come because He commanded us to watch and because we know He may come at any moment.

No One Knows or Can Know
When Christ Will Return

It is surprising and saddening to find how many ways people try to get around the repeated and plain statements of the Bible, that no one is to know when Christ may come. Despite repeated warnings that no one is to know the day, the hour, the time, the season, many people try to find evidences or inferences or signs by which they may foretell approximately or exactly when Jesus will come.

Perhaps half of the false cults are started by leaders who think they have some new knowledge about the time of the second coming. The Millerites and Seventh-Day Adventists tried to set the time encouraged by a misinterpretation of Daniel 8:14 and by a meteor shower, and first thought that Jesus would come in 1843. That date failing, then October 22, 1844. The British Israelites have set dates for Christ's coming judging by measurements in the great pyramid. Others have thought that they could make a day mean a year in the book of Daniel and so estimate when Christ should come. Martin Luther thought that the papacy was a sign of Christ's soon coming. Others have thought that the rise of Napoleon, of Kaiser Wilhelm, of Mussolini, of Hitler, of Stalin indicated the soon return of the Saviour. Every major flood, earthquake, or famine has been used as a sign. The rise of modernism, the rise of communism, of the false cults, have all been cited as evidences that Jesus must come by a certain time. The founding of the modern nation, Israel, is often so cited.

But all who try to prove by any signs or evidence that Christ will come within any specified time sin against the plain statements and the plain command of Jesus Christ. See again what Jesus said.

1. In the Olivet Discourse, Jesus Said That Neither Man Nor Angels, Nor He Himself Knew When He Would Return

In Matthew 24:36, speaking of the Second Coming, Jesus said, "But of that day and hour knoweth no man, no, not the angels of heaven, but my Father only."

In Mark 13:32, 33, we have Jesus' words as follows, "But of that day and that hour knoweth no man, no, not the angels which are in heaven, neither the Son, but the Father. Take ye heed, watch and pray: for ye know not when the time is."

Here we are told that "no man, no, not the angels which are in heaven, neither the Son," but only the Father knows when Christ will return! We believe that Christ now, in His exalted and glorious state, knows when He will return. But here I understand Him to claim that while on earth He did not know. If Jesus did not know, it was because He had emptied Himself of the outward evidences and marks of His deity. Certainly it is clear that no man in the world knows or can know when Christ will come and the angels themselves in Heaven do not know.

That means that there are no signs by which one can know, no way of figuring by the Bible, or of marking things by world events.

And again, in the next verse, Jesus solemnly warns, "Take ye heed, watch and pray: for ye know not when the time is."

Not only are we told that we do not know when the time of Christ's return is, but we are told that this is a part of the plan of God. It is a solemn duty to take heed, watch, and pray, and God has planned it this way so we will walk by faith and not by sight. God simply does not intend us to know when Christ will return.

By comparison of the Scripture in Matthew 24 and in Mark 13, we come upon another striking illustration given by the Saviour. In Matthew 24:43 and 44 we read the following statement: "But know this, that if the goodman of the house had known in what watch the thief would come, he would have watched, and would not have suffered his house to be broken up. Therefore be ye also ready: for in such hour as ye think not the Son of man cometh."

Here the illustration is used of a man, a householder, who has the misfortune of having a thief break into his house and steal. The point is that the coming of the Saviour will be as sudden, as unheralded and unexpected as the breaking in of a thief. And we are told that "the goodman of the house" will not know even what watch of the night, which of the three-hour periods into which the Roman night was divided, the thief would come. And the indication is that likewise we cannot even tell what watch it will be when Jesus comes.

This is a dark age in which we live. For the Christian, Christ is the bright and morning Star, a light in the darkness. When Jesus returns to reign on the earth, the darkness will be over, and so He is spoken of as "the Sun of righteousness" who will arise with healing in His wings for Israel. But this age is a dark age. It is the time of the Gentiles. The world is largely ruled by Satan, "the prince of the power of the air," who is called, "the god of this world." Now suppose that this long period between Christ's first coming and His second coming be divided into four watches. If it should turn out to be the year 2,000 before Jesus came, then each watch would be 500 years. And one cannot tell in which watch Jesus will come.

The same idea is expressed in the words of the Saviour in Mark 13:35, "Watch ye therefore: for ye know not when the master of the house cometh, at even, or at midnight, or at the cockcrowing, or in the morning." Here the four watches of the night are named; the Evening Watch, roughly from 6 P.M. till 9 P.M.; the Midnight Watch, which ends at midnight; the Cock-crowing Watch, ending at 3 A.M.; and the Morning Watch, ending at 6 A.M.

We learn that no man can know the day nor the hour when Jesus comes. But here we also learn that no one can even know the watch when Jesus will return. If the whole age should be divided into four parts, no one has any evidence by which they can foretell in which watch Jesus would return.

We do not know what watch it is even now, according to God's schedule, and we do not know when Christ will return. No one can know the day nor the hour or the century when Christ will return. But He may come at any moment.

2. *The Risen Saviour Warns the Apostles, "It Is Not for You to Know the Times or Seasons"*

We know how sorely tempted people are to try to set dates for Christ's coming. Evidently the apostles were as anxious about that as other men. After Jesus was risen from the dead, He talked to His disciples. "And, being assembled together with them, commanded them that they should not depart from Jerusalem, but wait for the promise of the Father, which, saith he, ye have heard of me. For John truly baptized with water; but ye shall be baptized with the Holy Ghost not many days hence" (Acts 1:4, 5).

Did the disciples now look forward to being filled with the Spirit and starting out to win souls? No, they did not. They immediately began to find out when Christ would return and set up the kingdom on earth, sitting on David's throne. "When they therefore were come together, they asked of him, saying, Lord, wilt thou at this time restore again the kingdom to Israel?" (Acts 1:6).

How many others would rather speculate on the time of Christ's return than to be filled with power and win souls! Now hear the Saviour's answer, "And he said unto them, It is not for you to know the times or the seasons, which the Father hath put in his own power" (Acts 1:7).

Jesus did not tell them when He would return. He did not say when He would set up the kingdom. In fact, He plainly told them, "It is not for you to know the times or the seasons, which the Father hath put in his own power." It is simply not God's plan for Christians to know the future!

The word *times* is used more than once in the Bible to represent years, and it may mean years here. In Daniel 7:25 we are told that the saints shall be given into the hand of the Antichrist "until a time and times and the dividing of time." These three and one-half years are clearly expressed elsewhere (Rev. 13:5; Rev. 11:2, 3). Revelation 12:14 also speaks of these three and one-half years as "a time, and times, and half a time." If one is not to know the time, then one is not to know even the year in which Christ will return.

And in Acts 1:7, Jesus said that one is not to know the season of Christ's return. I judge that this means some extended period of time. So we may safely say that one is not to know the day, or the hour, or the watch, or the year, or the era in which Jesus is to come.

The time of Christ's return is deliberately and intentionally left in the realm of the unrevealed. It is presumptuous for people to set out to know what God has plainly declared is not to be known.

Nearly all the fortunetellers play on this carnal longing to know the future. Nearly all the false cults some way appeal to men on this basis.

So the coming of Christ must be imminent. No signs need precede it. No preliminary warning comes of the end. No one can know when we are "in the closing days of the age." No one can know even approximately when Jesus will come. We are simply commanded to watch by faith and look for Christ's coming because He said to watch.

The Only "Signs" of Christ's Coming Will Be After the Rapture

We know from the Scripture that there will be two phases of Christ's coming. First, He will come into the air to receive His saints. At that time will occur the first resurrection, the living Christians will be changed, and all together will be caught up to meet the Lord in the air, and taken away for the wedding supper and the judgment seat of Christ in Heaven. On earth, meantime, will be a great tribulation. Then will come the second phase of Christ's Second Coming, when Christ will return with saints and angels, will appear on the Mount of Olives, with a mighty army of all the angels following Him. He will fight the Battle of Armageddon, set up His throne at Jerusalem, judge the Gentile nations, and reign for a thousand years. THE ONLY SIGNS MENTIONED IN THE BIBLE FOR CHRIST'S SECOND COMING REFER TO HIS REVELATION, WHEN HE COMES TO REIGN ON THE EARTH, IN THE SECOND PHASE OF HIS RETURN.

That, I believe, becomes evident on further study of the Scriptures.

I have been compelled to alter my previous position. During thirty years of ministry, I found that preaching on signs of Christ's Second Coming did not turn out satisfactorily. I once thought the rise of Mussolini might be a sign that the Roman Empire was about to be restored. I know now I was wrong. I have found that events which seemed very significant at the moment later faded into insignificance when Christ did not come when expected. I find that more and more false cults and heresies tend to arise out of stressing signs of Christ's coming. I find that preaching on signs of Christ's coming tends to cause people to sin by setting times or dates or approximate dates for Christ's return. More important, I find that the Bible doctrine of the imminency of Christ's coming does not fit with signs, and that in fact, we are not promised any signs whatever of the coming of Christ to receive His saints into the air! I am convinced that the only signs of Christ's coming mentioned in the Bible are the signs which must occur after Christ comes for His own at the rapture, signs which will occur during the tribulation time or afterward.

1. A Definitely Foretold, Measured, Scheduled Period of Time Like Daniel's Seventieth Week May Have Signs of the End; This Unscheduled, Undefinite Age May Not

The Bible tells us that after Christ comes into the air to receive His saints, there will be a seven-year period called Daniel's Seventieth week. In Daniel 9:24–27, we are told that seventy weeks of Jewish history were foretold. We are told, "Know therefore and understand, that from the going forth of the commandment to restore and to build Jerusalem unto the Messiah the Prince shall be seven weeks, and threescore and two weeks: the street shall be built again, and the wall, even in troublous times." Those sixty-nine weeks of years, 483 years, were fulfilled from the time of Ezra and Nehemiah, unto the coming of the Saviour. Then the Saviour was cut off, Jerusalem was destroyed, and the history of Jews as a nation lapsed. But after the rapture of the saints, the Man of Sin will make a covenant with the Jews for this last seventieth week of years. In the midst of that period, after three and one-half years, he will commit the "abomination of desolation" and begin his terrible persecution of the Jews. And this 3½ years, 42 months, 1,260 days, is called "the Great Tribulation."

See how definitely this period of time is outlined in the Bible. The first sixty-nine weeks have already been fulfilled, so we know that really they are weeks of years, or more literally, sevens of years. We do not know whether the prophesied covenant with the Jews by the Antichrist, a covenant for seven years, will be made immediately after the rapture, or a little later. But after that covenant is made, anybody left on the earth knowing the Scriptures ought to be able to count and find about when the

Lord Jesus would return to destroy the Antichrist and set up His kingdom on earth. We are told that the abomination of desolation, when the Man of Sin will claim to be God on earth, will happen "in the midst of the week" (Dan. 9:27). That will leave three and one-half years as the time when the Man of Sin or Antichrist will persecute the Jews and persecute the saints. This period is called "a time, and times, and the dividing of time," three and one-half years, in Daniel 7:25. It is the same 42 months of Revelation 11:2; the 1,260 days of Revelation 11:3, it is the "time, and times, and half a time," $3\frac{1}{2}$ years of persecution of "the woman," Israel, mentioned in Revelation 12:14; it is the 42 months in which the Antichrist will continue, mentioned in Revelation 13:5.

Obviously, after the rapture when Christ takes His saints into the air, we shall enter into a scheduled period of time well outlined. Recently as I rode a Pennsylvania train from Chicago to Lancaster, Pennsylvania, I could tell when we approached Lancaster by the stations we went through. We were at Pittsburgh about nine o'clock, and I knew we were hours away from our destination. But later we passed Johnstown; we were getting nearer. At Altoona, I knew that time was shorter. When we arrived at Harrisburg, I knew that the next stop of the fast train would be Lancaster. You see, on approaching a scheduled and timed event, one can see the end approaching. In that case there are signs of the end, or milestones.

However, such is not the case in this present age. There are no milestones to go by, saying that the end is coming, because the end is promised to come suddenly, without warning, so that no man can know when it approaches. If the coming of Christ be imminent, that is, that Jesus may come at any time, without any preliminary warning, without any scheduling of previous events, then there can be no signs of Christ's coming into the air to receive His saints. This coming of Christ into the air to receive us is to be as sudden as the coming of the unexpected flood in Noah's day, as sudden as a thief coming in the night, so that the goodman does not know what watch of the night the thief will come. It is to be like a master unexpectedly returning in the midst of the night from a long journey. We are to watch because there will be no warning, no sign, no preliminary events to warn us.

For example, if Jesus could have come in Paul's day, and if Paul was right to expect His coming and to teach the Thessalonians to "wait for his Son from heaven" (I Thess. 1:10), then it is obvious that World War I, or World War II, or the return of the handful of Jews to Palestine, could not be signs of that coming! The coming of Christ to receive His saints is an unscheduled matter, the time is kept secret, and there are no events which can herald the approach of Christ's coming.

We will be saved grief, heresy, and trouble if we will remember the thing the dear Saviour stressed the most, "Watch therefore: for ye know not what hour your Lord doth come" (Matt. 24:42).

2. The Signs Promised by the Saviour in the Olivet Discourse Are to Follow the Rapture, Not to Precede It

How many thousands of preachers preach sermons on "Signs of Christ's Coming"! So did I. But I was wrong, because I misunderstood some Scriptures and did not look closely enough to see what they said.

In the Olivet Discourse, as recorded in Matthew 24, let us see what questions were asked Jesus and what He really promised.

First, read what Jesus said and the disciples' questions.

"And Jesus said unto them, See ye not all these things? verily I say unto you, There shall not be left here one stone upon another, that shall not be thrown down. And as he sat upon the mount of Olives, the disciples came unto him privately, saying, Tell us, when shall these things be? and what shall be the sign of thy coming, and of the end of the world?"—Matt. 24:2, 3.

Note the two questions: 1. "When shall these things be?" that is, the destruction of the temple and Jerusalem. Obviously, this happened in A.D. 40, and is already passed. 2. "What shall be the sign of thy coming, and of the end of the world?"

The question as recorded in Mark 13:4, is, "Tell us, when shall these things be? and what shall be the sign when all these things shall be fulfilled?"

Now which phase of Christ's coming is meant in this question?

Are the disciples asking about when the rapture will take place, when Christ will come into the air, when we shall be caught up to meet Him? Or are they speaking about His return to reign, when His feet shall stand upon the Mount of Olives, when He shall destroy the enemies of the Jews and set up His kingdom at Jerusalem?

Naturally, Jews would be more concerned with the revelation of Christ, His literal descent to the earth to regather all the Jews and save them and re-establish David's throne at Jerusalem. Throughout the Old Testament the prophecies about Christ's Second Coming are nearly always concerned with this second phase of His return when He is to come all the way down to the earth and regather Israel, save them and restore the Jewish kingdom. The rapture is scarcely mentioned in the Old Testament and we can see why.

When these same apostles asked Jesus about His return in Acts 1:6, they said, "Lord, wilt thou at this time restore again the kingdom to Israel?" That question is only a few days after this one in the Olivet Discourse. You see, it is the return of Christ after the tribulation, *with* saints and angels, which is meant here.

That is made specially clear because the question has two parts. "What shall be the sign of thy coming, and of the end of the world?" Perhaps that ought to be translated, "the end of the age." That means the end of Gentile rule, the times of the Gentiles. And this age will not end at the rapture, but after the tribulation time, when Christ sets up His kingdom on earth. So the sign of Christ's coming mentioned in Matthew 24:3 is a sign of His coming in power and glory, bringing us back with Him *after the tribulation.*

That is the way Jesus answered the question, too. Later in the chapter we read:

"Immediately after the tribulation of those days shall the sun be darkened, and the moon shall not give her light, and the stars shall fall from heaven, and the powers of the heavens shall be shaken: And then shall appear the sign of the Son of man in heaven: and then shall all the tribes of the earth mourn, and they shall see the Son of man coming in the clouds of heaven with power and great glory.—Matt. 24:29, 30.

After the tribulation, that is, after we have been caught up in the air to meet Christ and have gone with Him to Heaven, after Daniel's seventieth week is finished, after the tribulation is over, then will appear "the sign of the Son of man in heaven" and people shall "see the Son of man coming in the clouds of heaven with power and great glory."

In the tribulation time, anybody who is left here, converted in that time and called to preach, might well preach on the signs of Christ's coming. But now there are to be no signs until after the rapture, and after we shall be taken to Heaven.

3. There Is No Prophetic Significance in the Present Partial Worldly Establishment of a Jewish State in Israel

Thousands of Christians suppose that when a handful of unconverted Jews by worldly methods seized part of Palestine and part of Jerusalem and were proclaimed a separate nation May 14, 1948, that that was a definite sign that Christ must come soon.

But they base that teaching on a misunderstanding of what Jesus said in that Olivet Discourse, as I will show you.

Now read Matthew 24:29–33:

"Immediately after the tribulation of those days shall the sun be darkened, and the moon shall not give her light, and the stars shall fall from heaven, and the powers of the heavens shall be shaken: And then shall appear the sign of the Son of man in heaven: and then shall all the tribes of the earth mourn, and they shall see the Son of man coming in the clouds of heaven with power and great glory. And he shall send his angels with a great sound of a trumpet, and they shall gather together his elect from the four winds, from one end of heaven to the other. Now learn a parable of the fig tree; When his branch is yet tender, and putteth forth leaves, ye know that summer is nigh: So likewise ye, when ye shall see all these things, know that it is near, even at the doors."

I wanted you to see those verses all together. Note that everything in these verses happens "immediately AFTER THE TRIBULATION." The things prophesied here do not happen before Christ comes to call us out to meet Him at the rapture. Rather, they come after the tribulation time.

Someone says that the fig tree in the Bible always represents Israel; therefore the establishment of Israel as a nation is a sign that Christ must come.

But here we see that these words are not for our times at all. The present small and partial establishment of the nation Israel in unbelief is an entirely different matter from the tremendous, miraculous event which is foretold in the Bible. When Christ comes to the earth bodily, in glory, to set up His kingdom, "immediately after the tribulation," His sign will appear in Heaven, and all men shall see it coming. Then "he shall send his angels with a great sound of a trumpet, and they shall gather together his elect [Israel, the chosen nation, all the Jews left alive in the world] from the four winds, from one end of heaven to the other." Note that this regathering is to be miraculous, is to be done by the angels of God, and is to be complete. Every Jew in the world will be miraculously regathered to Palestine.

If you will read the Old Testament prophecy of this event in Deuteronomy 30:1-6, you will see that every Jew will be regathered miraculously, that every one will be circumcised in heart, that is, born again, and all will be brought "into the land which thy fathers possessed," Palestine. But no such miraculous and universal regathering of Israel has yet taken place. The prophecy has not been fulfilled. It will be fulfilled "immediately after the tribulation." What has happened in Palestine is not the prophesied event which will come later, after we are caught up to meet the Lord in the air and when we return with Him to reign.

So when we speak of signs of Christ's coming, we ought to mean signs that will occur after we have been caught up with Christ in the air, after the tribulation.

4. Daniel's "Time of the End" Does Not Refer to Our Day, but to the Tribulation Time

In Daniel 12:4 are these words often misunderstood by those who preach on signs of Christ's coming. We read, "But thou, O Daniel, shut up the words, and seal the book, even to the time of the end: many shall run to and fro, and knowledge shall be increased."

Many people suppose that the truth about preliminary events

before Christ should return to catch away His bride were hidden from people in Daniel's time, but would be revealed in "the time of the end." And such good Christians often suppose that the term "the time of the end" or "the end time" refers to the last few years of this church age, before Christ shall come into the air to receive His saints. But they are wrong. "The time of the end" refers to the tribulation time.

In the Scofield Bible is a very clear and helpful note on this question. On page 919, Dr. Scofield says:

"The 'time of the end' in Daniel. The expression, or its equivalent, 'in the end,' occurs, Dan. 8:17–19; 9:26; 11:35, 40, 45; 12:4, 6, 9. Summary: (1) The time of the end in Daniel begins with the violation by 'the prince that shall come' (i.e. 'little horn,' 'man of sin,' 'Beast') of his covenant with the Jews for the restoration of the temple and sacrifice (Dan. 9:27), and his presentation of himself as God (Dan. 9:27; 11:36–38; Matt. 24:15; II Thess. 2:4; Rev. 13:4–6), and ends with his destruction by the appearing of the Lord in glory (II Thess. 2:8; Rev. 19:19, 20). (2) The duration of the 'time of the end' is three and one half years, coinciding with the last half of the seventieth week of Daniel (Dan. 7:25; 12:7; Rev. 13:5). (3) This 'time of the end' is the 'time of Jacob's trouble' (Jer. 30:7); 'a time of trouble such as never was since there was a nation' (Dan. 12:1); 'great tribulation such as was not from the beginning of the world . . . nor ever shall be' (Matt. 24:21). The N. T., especially the Book of the Revelation, adds many details."

A careful study of the Scriptures mentioned will convince one that Daniel's "time of the end" is the tribulation period, and that none of the things mentioned are signs to us who live now and will be called out to meet Christ before the tribulation begins.

5. The Preaching of the Gospel to All the World Now Could Not Be a Sign of Christ's Coming

Some are wrong in supposing that Matthew 24:14 refers to this present time. In my humble judgment, one is entirely wrong to suppose that the present-day preaching of the Gospel in all the world, now, is referred to in verse 14.

In the first place, the Gospel has already been preached in all the world, long, long ago, and that is not a peculiar sign of this age. The Gospel was preached in all the world, even in apostolic times. At Pentecost, we are told, "And there were dwelling at

Jerusalem Jews, devout men, out of every nation under heaven," and these had the Gospel preached to them, and in turn they preached it to their people. In Romans 1:8, Paul says, "First, I thank my God through Jesus Christ for you all, that your faith is spoken of throughout the whole world." If the whole world had heard of the Christian faith of the saints at Rome, then the whole world had heard the Gospel. And in Colossians 1:5 and 6, Paul speaks of ". . . the gospel; Which is come unto you, as it is in all the world . . ." So all the world had already heard the Gospel in apostolic times.

In the second place, in Matthew 24:14, Jesus clearly had in mind the end of the age, that is, the "times of the Gentiles," and that end of the age, or the end of the world about which the disciples asked in verse 3, will not come until after the rapture, after the tribulation, after the return of Christ in glory with saints and angels, and after the battle of Armageddon, with the setting up of Christ's throne. It is during the tribulation time that the Gospel of the kingdom will be preached in all the world, again, and then will come the end of the tribulation and the end of the age. So the preaching of the Gospel now in all the world could not possibly be a sign of Christ's coming.

Some Other So-Called Signs Are Only Characteristics of This Whole Age

In His discourse on the Mount of Olives concerning His Second Coming, Jesus gave the disciples plain warning that they should not be deceived about signs of His coming.

1. Wars, Famines, Pestilences, Earthquakes, False Cults Are Characteristics of This Whole Age, Not Signs of Christ's Second Coming

When Jesus started to answer their question, "Tell us, when shall these things be? and what shall be the sign of thy coming, and of the end of the world?" (Matt. 24:3), this is the warning He gave them:

"And Jesus answered and said unto them, Take heed that no man deceive you. For many shall come in my name, saying, I

*am Christ; and shall deceive many. And ye shall hear of wars
and rumours of wars: see that ye be not troubled: for all these
things must come to pass, but the end is not yet. For nation shall
rise against nation, and kingdom against kingdom: and there
shall be famines, and pestilences, and earthquakes, in divers
places"*—Matt. 24:4–7.

Jesus names a number of things here, including wars, famines,
pestilences, earthquakes, etc., but He makes clear "for all these
things must come to pass, BUT THE END IS NOT YET"! The
things named here are not signs of the second coming. Rather,
they are characteristics of the whole age!

We think that modern war is terrible. Actually more people
died for the number engaged in the Civil War in America than
in World Wars I or II. The Thirty Years' War in Europe was
more destructive of life in the area covered than other wars since
that time in Europe. The destruction of Jerusalem and the dispersion of the Jewish nation a few years after Jesus gave these
words was infinitely more terrible than has happened to any
single nation since that time. Wars, famines, pestilences, earthquakes are simply characteristics of this whole age and ought not
to be counted as signs of Christ's Second Coming.

I am very familiar with the interpretation some give that the
last two so-called world wars were "global" and that the others
before were not. Actually, of course, there is a sense in which the
Thirty Years' War in Europe involved most of the nations of
the world. The Napoleonic Wars involved Europe, Africa, Asia,
and Mexico. The wars of Caesar and of Alexander the Great involved three continents. Then it is equally true that World Wars I
and II did not involve every nation in the earth. The difference
in the wars was in degree but not essentially in kind. I believe
that one has no right to say that Matthew 24:6 and 7 taken at its
face value pictures "global wars" that would not picture the wars
before World War I.

In fact "nation shall rise against nation, and kingdom against
kingdom" simply states that one nation will rise against another
nation, and one kingdom shall rise against another kingdom.
There is not even a hint here of a global war as such, or universal

war. That very popular interpretation, it seems to me, is stretched to meet the needs of the theory, but that interpretation is not inherent in the Scripture itself.

Can you say that a war is global if it does not involve all the nations? Is it total war which leaves untouched the scores of nations in South America, much of Africa, and much of Asia? At very best, the participation of a majority of the nations in the last World War was only a token participation, and did not seriously threaten the nations or occupy much of their manpower or resources or essentially immediately concern their destiny. The war was bad, but so are all wars.

Again, it goes against the context to say that in Matthew 24:4–7 Jesus is speaking at all of any signs of His second coming. Only one "sign" was mentioned in the question (verse 3), and only one "sign" is mentioned in Christ's answer (verse 30). The disciples said, "Tell us, when shall these things be? and what shall be the sign of thy coming, and of the end of the world?" Notice it is only one sign mentioned. And Jesus answers that in the same chapter, verses 29 and 30. He says, "Immediately after the tribulation . . . then shall appear the sign of the Son of man in heaven." So the single sign here discussed in Matthew 24 will occur after the tribulation, and therefore after the rapture.

Neither the question nor the answer referred to the wars, false cults, famines, pestilences, and earthquakes mentioned in these verses, 4 to 7. These verses describe the course of the age, and Jesus plainly says that "for all these things must come to pass, but the end is not yet." They are not to be regarded as signs of Christ's coming. They are simply the marks of the whole age, concerning which Jesus plainly warns us that we are not to be deceived.

2. The Term "the Last Days" in the Bible Refers to this Whole Age, Not Simply to a Few Years Preceding Christ's Coming

A number of times in the New Testament, terms are used referring to a certain period as "the last days" or "the latter times." People have sometimes supposed that such terms refer to closing days or years of this age, just preceding Christ's coming into the air for His saints. So I Timothy 1:4, speaking of "the latter times," is supposed to give a sign of Christ's coming. Second

Timothy 3:1–5 is supposed by some to picture the terrible apostasy just before Christ returns, because it mentions "in the last days." Second Peter 3:3 mentions "in the last days" scoffers who will deny the second coming. This is regarded as a sign that Christ must soon come.

But all these inferences are not justified by the Scriptures because the term "the last days" in the New Testament refers to this whole age, that is, the New Testament age instead of the Old Testament age. The term refers to this age of the Great Commission, the age of the church, instead of the age of the ceremonial law. That is easy to prove.

In Acts 2:14–21 we find Peter standing up at Pentecost and explaining the miraculous happenings of that day. He said:

> "But this is that which was spoken by the prophet Joel: And it shall come to pass IN THE LAST DAYS, saith God, I will pour out of my Spirit upon all flesh: and your sons and your daughters shall prophesy, and your young men shall see visions, and your old men shall dream dreams"—vss. 16, 17.

The pouring out of the Holy Spirit at Pentecost partially marks the fulfillment of that prophecy, says Peter, by divine inspiration. So *the last days* must include the Pentecostal revival, and go on through until "that great and notable day of the Lord" (vs. 20). "The last days" means this whole age. Scriptures that tell of what will happen in the last days or the latter times mean certain characteristics of this whole age.

Again in Hebrews 1:1 and 2 we read a definitive passage of Scripture about the "last days":

> "God, who at sundry times and in divers manners spake in time past unto the fathers by the prophets, Hath IN THESE LAST DAYS spoken unto us by his Son, whom he hath appointed heir of all things, by whom also he made the worlds."

Jesus Christ's public ministry began the last days. The last days included Pentecost. The last days go on through this age till "the day of the Lord," as we saw in Acts 2:20. Thus the Bible passages referring to the last days do not mean a few closing days or years before Christ comes, but the whole age. So the events or conditions mentioned could not be signs of Christ's coming. Further study of every passage in the New Testament with the term "the last days" or its equivalent will show that the time then present was meant.

Another interesting passage which bears on this question is I John 2:18:

"Little children, it is the last time: and as ye have heard that antichrist shall come, even now are there many antichrists; whereby we know that it is the last time."

It was already "the last time" when John wrote his epistle. So the term "the last time" or "the last days" or "the latter times" refers to the whole age, and what people have thought were conditions which must immediately precede Christ's coming, are really conditions during the whole age, and have nothing to do with signs of Christ's coming.

Yet Other Scriptures Are Sometimes Misunderstood to Mark Signs That Will Precede Christ's Coming

Perhaps in one brief chapter we cannot answer every question, but there are yet two other Scriptures which have been misunderstood, and so have been used as a basis for preaching the signs of Christ's coming.

1. The "Great Apostasy," Supposed to Come Just Before Christ Returns, Is a Result of a Misunderstood Scripture

Second Thessalonians 2:1-3 speaks of "a falling away" which is supposed to come before the day of the Lord, that is, before Christ returns to reign. Let us read the passage prayerfully.

"Now we beseech you, brethren, by the coming of our Lord Jesus Christ, and by our gathering together unto him, That ye be not soon shaken in mind, or be troubled, neither by spirit, nor by word, nor by letter as from us, as that the day of Christ is at hand. Let no man deceive you by any means: for that day shall not come, except there come a falling away first, and that man of sin be revealed, the son of perdition."

Some Thessalonians had misunderstood Paul's first letter, perhaps, and they thought that the day of the Lord, when Christ will return to regather Israel and reign on the earth, was to come immediately. No, Paul wrote them by divine inspiration that certain other things must occur first before the reign of Christ. These things are numbered: (1) "the falling away," first; (2) "And that man of sin will be revealed." We are told that these two things must come before Christ returns to fight the Battle of Armageddon, regather the Jews, and reign on David's throne. There must come a falling away and a Man of Sin, the Antichrist, must appear, bringing with him, of course, the Great Tribulation.

Then we are told a little further that "the mystery of iniquity doth already work: only he who now letteth will let, until he be taken out of the way. And then shall that Wicked be revealed . . ."

Now it has come about naturally that many people thought that "a falling away" mentioned here is a spiritual apostasy. In fact in the margin of the Scofield Reference Bible is a note which says "the apostasy." And that idea comes from a very curious truth. The Greek word here is literally *apostasy*. The English word apostasy is not a translation, but a transliteration of the word. However, people are misled by this fact because the word in the Greek does not necessarily mean the same as apostasy means in English. In the Greek it means a loosing, a falling away; and so the King James translators properly translated it "a falling away."

It often occurs that when a word goes from one language to another it has a greatly modified meaning. For example, the Greek word *dunamis* came over into the English language as dynamite. But it does not mean dynamite in the Greek at all; it means power and is the word used in Acts 1:8, "ye shall receive power."

Another illustration is our English word impediment. It is really a Latin word, brought over into the English language. But in the Latin it means army baggage, as one who has studied Caesar's Gallic Wars might remember. The baggage was in the way in fighting and so it came to mean an impediment, a hindrance; but that is not the literal meaning in the Latin.

So the Greek word for falling away does not mean necessarily apostasy.

Then what does it mean? It seems to me to definitely mean the rapture of the saints. One of these days the pull of gravity that binds us to this earth will be loosed in a moment, and we will be caught up to meet the Lord Jesus in the air. We will literally fall away from the earth to meet Jesus Christ. And this literal meaning fits the Greek fully as well if not better than to spiritualize the word and make it mean a falling away from Christ or doctrine.

Besides, this meaning is necessary. Look again at II Thessalonians 2:3. Two conditions must be fulfilled before Christ comes to reign on earth. Those two conditions are the falling away and the Man of Sin with his persecutions and tribulations for the earth. But what about the rapture of the saints? Must not that come first? If the coming of Christ is imminent, and may come at any moment; if Christ's coming into the air to receive His saints is the next thing on God's program, then certainly the rapture must come before Christ's return to reign. If you make "a falling away" mean Christians falling away from this earth, caught up to meet Christ in the air, then the picture is complete. Without this you have an apostasy coming before Christ's reign, and the Man of Sin coming before Christ's reign, but nothing about the rapture at all!

Yet later in the same passage, the rapture is inferred, because the Holy Spirit is said to now hinder the coming of the Antichrist and his wickedness, until He, the Holy Spirit, be taken out of the way. The Holy Spirit will doubtless be caught up in the bodies of believers, and in that sense, He will no longer hinder the appearance of the Man of Sin. But the rapture is not mentioned as one of the things preceding the day of the Lord unless "a falling away" refers to the rapture, as I believe it clearly does.

How could Christ's coming be imminent, if Christ could not come until the theory of evolution became popular? Or how could Christ's coming be imminent, so that He might have come even in New Testament times, if He could not come before modernism gained such headway in certain American denominations? No, it simply doesn't fit. Apostasy in doctrine is no sign of Christ's coming. There are no signs by which anybody can know when the coming of the Saviour approaches. And II Thessalonians 2:3

says that the rapture itself must precede the coming of the day of the Lord. Properly speaking, the only two things that precede the "day of the Lord" are the rapture and the Man of Sin with all the entails.

Apostasy? It happened in the first and second centuries so that not a single one of the churches mentioned as the seven churches of Asia in Revelation, chapters 2 and 3, now remain. Rome, with all her heresy, developed centuries ago.

Does any reader believe that the awful apostasy which almost put out the Gospel light for centuries in the Dark Ages was preferable to the apostasy today? Does any one believe that the Spanish Inquisition, the burnings at the stake, the massacre of whole cities and peoples was essentially better than modernism and false cults today? The simple truth is that the tendency of poor, carnal human hearts to fall away from the truth is inherent in the race and happens in all ages. Apostasy was as much current in the seven churches of Asia as it is current today in American denominations. Those who think that modernism and worldliness are new manifestations have simply not learned from the Bible how wicked is the human heart in all ages, and have not learned from history how depravity thus has showed itself in every century.

Apostasy is not a mark of the close of the age, and has nothing prophetically to do with the second coming of Christ. We are to expect the dear Saviour to come at any time, signs or no signs, because He said He would, and because He commanded us to watch.

2. The Warning of Hebrews 10:25, "As Ye See the Day Approaching" Told the Jews in Jerusalem of the Near Destruction of the City in A.D. 70

Once I supposed that Hebrews 10:25 spoke of the Second Coming. It says, "Not forsaking the assembling of ourselves together, as the manner of some is; but exhorting one another: and so much the more, as ye see the day approaching." However, on making a more thorough study of the book of Hebrews, I became convinced that this is a warning of the coming destruction of the city of Jerusalem which occurred in A.D. 70, at the hand of Titus and his Roman army.

We remember that Jesus had given most solemn warning of this coming ruin to the city He loved.

"And when ye shall see Jerusalem compassed with armies, then know that the desolation thereof is nigh. Then let them which are in Judaea flee to the mountains; and let them which are in the midst of it depart out; and let not them that are in the countries enter thereinto. For these be the days of vengeance, that all things which are written may be fulfilled. But woe unto them that are with child, and to them that give suck, in those days! for there shall be great distress in the land, and wrath upon this people. And they shall fall by the edge of the sword, and shall be led away captive into all nations: and Jerusalem shall be trodden down of the Gentiles, until the times of the Gentiles be fulfilled."
—Luke 21:20–24.

This destruction occurred A.D. 70, about thirty-seven years after Jesus made this prediction.

Later the book of Hebrews takes up the same kind of solemn warning. When the book of Hebrews was written, the temple seems to have been still standing in Jerusalem, the Levites and priests carrying on the regular sacrifices. Hebrews 10:11 says, "And every priest standeth daily ministering and offering oftentimes the same sacrifices, which can never take away sins." Note the present tense of that Scripture. The sacrifices were still being offered in the temple when the book of Hebrews was written.

Note also Hebrews 7:9 which says, "And as I may so say, Levi also, who receiveth tithes, payed tithes in Abraham." The priests and Levites, descendants of Levi, were even then receiving tithes in the temple at Jerusalem. And verse 5 in the same chapter says, "And verily they that are of the sons of Levi, who receive the office of the priesthood, have a commandment to take tithes of the people according to the law . . ."

Note also Hebrews 13:10, "We have an altar, whereof they have no right to eat which serve the tabernacle." Priests and Levites even then, when the book of Hebrews was written, ate of other sacrifices brought to the temple at Jerusalem. So the book of Hebrews was written shortly before the destruction of Jerusalem, probably A.D. 64.

Now throughout the book of Hebrews, Jews were being prepared for the final dissolution of all the temple sacrifices and services. Hebrews tells how Christ is better than angels, how Christ is better than Moses, how Christ is better than the high priests of Israel, how the sacrifice made by Christ once and for all purchased salvation, as the animal sacrifices could not do. We are told how the new covenant supersedes the old covenant and the old is ready to pass away. Then we are told in Hebrews, chapter 9, how the blood of Christ is infinitely superior to the blood of goats and calves, and the heavenly sanctuary is infinitely better than the temple at Jerusalem. Finally all this teaching comes to a mighty climax in Hebrews 10:18, "Now where remission of these is, there is no more offering for sin."

The Old Testament sacrifices are over. The temple will be destroyed, the priesthood scattered, the animal sacrifices offered no more! For now, through Christ, we have boldness to enter into the holiest by the blood of Jesus, we are told. If you will read Hebrews 10:18-25 with this in mind, you will see how God brings the subject to the mighty climax. The believers among the Jews are solemnly warned to meet together to exhort one another, to hold fast the profession of faith without wavering, as they see the armies gathering about Jerusalem and the inevitable destruction of it, as foretold by Jesus Christ, about to take place! ". . . so much the more as ye see the day approaching."

Now after building up to the mention of destruction in Hebrews 10:25, verses 26-31 speak of the vengeance of God, His judgment and fiery indignation, and of sinners dying without mercy who have trodden under foot the Son of God. God's vengeance is coming! "It is a fearful thing to fall into the hands of the living God" (Heb. 10:31).

Thereafter, properly enough, the rest of the book of Hebrews leaves off the discussion of the Hebrew temple, sacrifices, covenant and priesthood to speak of the heroes of the faith, of trial, and testing, and martyrdom, and chastening. And the one place which mentions again the Jewish altars and sacrifices is in Hebrews 13:10-14, which tells these Jewish Christians solemnly, "Let us go forth therefore unto him without the camp, bearing his reproach. For here have we no continuing city, but we seek one to come" (vss. 13, 14). Jerusalem will be destroyed. These converted Jews will be wanderers on the face of the earth now, without any continuing city, and so they are told that they may bear the solemn reproach of Christ and look for another city, when Jesus comes!

A solemn study of Hebrews 10:25, in view of the whole book, seems to me conclusive proof that when Paul, by divine inspiration, warned the Hebrew people, ". . . but exhorting one another: and so much the more, as ye see the day approaching" he was warning them of the destruction of Jerusalem which Jesus had clearly foretold and which was to occur within a short time. He was not warning of the second coming of Christ.

Nobody will "see the day approaching" when Jesus will come. Multiplied thousands have thought they saw it, but were mistaken. Martin Luther thought he saw it when he rushed his book on Daniel into print before the Saviour should come. The Millerites thought they saw it with the shower of meteors which they thought fulfilled prophecy and portended the coming of the Saviour. "Pastor" Russell thought he saw the day of Christ approaching, and solemnly promised that Christ would come in 1914, but he was mistaken. No, we do not "see the day approaching" of Christ's coming. But Jews saw solemn portents of terrifying signs that the city of Jerusalem would be destroyed. And the book of Hebrews was written partly to prepare Jewish believers for the utter destruction of the temple and its sacrifices and the scattering of its priesthood.

When Jesus said ". . . The kingdom of God cometh not with observation" (Luke 17:20), He certainly did not mean that people could see His coming approaching, but the contrary, as the context shows.

When Jesus said, "No man knoweth the day nor the hour wherein the Son of man cometh" He certainly meant that we could not see the day of His coming approaching.

The Danger and Harm of Date-Setting and Sign-Watching

A deep concern has come upon me as I have seen the results of setting out to find signs on every hand for Christ's coming, and practically setting dates for Christ's return.

First of all, Jesus plainly said not to do it. He said concerning His Second Coming, ". . . It is not for you to know the times or the seasons, which the Father hath put in his own power" (Acts 1:7).

Again He plainly said, ". . . The kingdom of God cometh not with observation" (Luke 17:20). That is, Jesus said, no one can now observe the approach of the kingdom. There are no signs, no preliminary events by which anyone can judge how near is Christ's coming. Surely we must be impressed with the thought that one who seeks to know what Jesus plainly said we were not to know, sins against the Saviour.

Such setting of dates tends to heresy. I call your attention to Jehovah's Witnesses, the Seventh-Day Adventists, the British Israelites, and all the other groups who pretend to know that we are in the very closing days of the age, and who claim they have special revelation concerning it which other cults do not have. The so-called Latter Rain is such a heresy. Currently there is a great turning of heretofore sound Bible teachers to believe that the church must go through the tribulation. They are "restudying prophecy," they say. The simple truth is that they have set so many signs, and then found their prophecies were not fulfilled and Christ did not come, until now many choose to believe that they were right about it being the closing days of the age, but they believe the tribulation time is simply coming on without the rapture, and that saved people will go through the tribulation. In this they sin against the clear Bible teaching of the imminence of Christ's coming.

Again, all this preaching on signs tends to put the emphasis on the newspaper instead of on the Bible. It tends to teach a doctrine depending on sight instead of depending on faith. Also, it cultivates a certain sensationalism, a clamoring for attention by bizarre and strange interpretations. Preachers are spending much time preaching on the atomic bomb, on Russia, on the coming world war III, and political alliances with other nations, on "the kings of the east," instead of preaching Bible truths. How many have accused evangelists of being sensational because they preach on sin, Hell, and judgment! On these, good evangelists ought to create a sensation. But it is infinitely worse to be sensational about simple worldly current events, trying to give them some eternal and prophetic significance beyond what the Bible speaks. That is wrong.

This looking for signs, this preaching that we are in the closing days is a discouraging business. It leads people to believe we can have no more great revivals. It leads to defeatism in prayer and labor. It discourages soul winning.

And one terrible result of all this speculation, and theorizing, and sign-finding, and date-setting is that great reproach is brought on the blessed scriptural doctrine of the premillennial return of Jesus Christ.

Let us come back to the Bible emphasis, brethren. Let all of us come back to teach and preach again, and warn our own hearts repeatedly that Jesus is coming, that no one knows when, and that we are to solemnly watch and wait and look for His coming as a matter of simple faith because He said to do it.

Signs there will be in the tribulation time, especially signs for the Jews, ". . . the Jews require a sign . . ." (I Cor. 1:22). But this day does not require a sign; it requires faithful obedience to the plain word of Jesus Christ. We are to be like the faithful porter waiting to open the door to the returning master, however late his coming. Jesus may come today. He may not come for a thousand years. But we can hope for His coming now, and be ready at any moment while we do His will.

Chapter 15

Get Ready for Christ's Coming

SINCE JESUS is coming, I beseech you to get ready. The wise virgins had oil in their lamps; the foolish had no oil and were left behind. Jesus said, "Be ye therefore ready."

First of all, those who know they are saved should so live that they will not be ashamed before Christ at His coming. This duty of all Christians to be ready for Jesus is expressed in I John 2:28, which says, "And now, little children, abide in him; that, when he shall appear, we may have confidence, and not be ashamed before him at his coming." I know I am saved, and therefore when Jesus comes, I will go with Him. But a child of God who is not on duty, not winning souls, not living right will be ashamed before Christ when He comes.

We will go with Christ to the wedding supper, but we should also remember that we go to the judgment seat of Christ. We must give an account of our stewardship and receive our reward. One for his faithfulness is to rule over ten cities, and another over five cities (Luke 19:17–19). We are to be rewarded every man according to his works. But our works shall be tried by fire (I Cor. 3:12–15). Our works may be gold, silver, and precious stones, beautiful things that abide, or they may be wood, hay, and stubble, temporary things that will burn and be destroyed. First Corinthians 3:14, 15 says: "If any man's work abide which he hath built thereupon, he shall receive a reward. If any man's work shall be burned, he shall suffer loss: but he himself shall be saved; yet so as by fire."

Even a child of God, saved by the blood, who is caught up to meet Christ in the air but finds all of his works burned up and with no treasures in Heaven, will be ashamed before Christ at His coming. I am not talking now about salvation, for that is

forever settled when one believes on Christ. Salvation is given alike to all who trust in Christ and on the merits of the shed blood of Jesus. But after our bodies are glorified and after we are entered into everlasting life, then those who have labored well will have their rewards, and those who have none will be ashamed before Jesus at His coming! Then Christian, do not waste the hours, but redeem the time, for the coming of the Lord draweth nigh!

I recall some years ago in Fort Worth, Texas, a man had lost his little son twelve years old. It had been my privilege to win the boy to Christ, and the mother and father clung to me for comfort in their loss. I remember that the father came to me and told me how he had found the little boy's toys in the garage, lying where he had left them when he went suddenly and unexpectedly home to be with God. Then the father said to me, "Brother Rice, I have just realized that this business that I have built up and all my property and my interests here on earth are nothing but toys. One day I will go away and leave them just as my son left his skates and wagon and ball and bat."

Dear brother, the things that are seen are temporal, but the things that are unseen are eternal. Jesus is coming! Let us lay up treasures in Heaven while we can, and then we will not be ashamed before Him when He comes.

Get Unsaved Loved Ones Ready

Several years ago after I had preached in a great church several times on the second coming of Christ, I went through the audience as they waited for a baptismal service, and a woman plucked me by the sleeve. I looked down and the tears were running down her face. Her voice trembled as she said, "Brother Rice, do you think Jesus is coming soon?"

I answered, "I do not know, but I hope and believe that He is. There are many signs that Jesus is likely to come soon. Why do you ask?"

"Oh, I am afraid He is!" she said. "You and others have been preaching on the Second Coming, and I have been reading my Bible, and I am afraid He is coming soon."

"Why are you afraid?" I asked. "Aren't you a Christian? Wouldn't you be glad to see Him?"

"Oh, I am ready myself," she said, "but my husband is lost, and I am afraid Jesus will come before he is saved, and I will have to leave him behind."

I urged the dear woman to do what she could to win her husband now. Her tears and her deep concern over her husband impressed me greatly. We talk about how terrible it would be for a sinner to be left behind when Jesus comes, and that is true. But we must not forget that much of the responsibility is on us. If you who read this have loved ones unsaved, I beg you, do your best to get them saved now. Jesus said, "I must work the works of him that sent me, while it is day: the night cometh, when no man can work" (John 9:4). So let us win them while we can.

One of the greatest joys of my heart as I look forward to the rapture and the meeting of Christ in the air is the thought of seeing those whom God has helped me win to Christ. That is what Paul meant, too, when he said in I Thessalonians, "For what is our hope, or joy, or crown of rejoicing? Are not even ye in the presence of our Lord Jesus Christ at his coming?" (I Thess. 2:19). I want to see Jesus first, of course, see the scars in His hands and kiss His feet. But then I want to see them as they meet Jesus, those to whom God has let me preach the gospel, those whose hands I have taken as they have taken Christ, those who came with penitent tears and surrendered hearts in country brush-arbors, in churches, in tents and tabernacles, open-air and theatre meetings all up and down this land! Oh! what a joy when I see them everyone greet the Saviour to whom I first introduced them in my poor ministry! That is my crown of rejoicing! That is my glory and joy when Jesus comes. And I want to win as many as I can, knowing that my joy and my reward at the coming of Christ will depend largely on how many others I have brought to Jesus.

But Are You, Yourself, Ready to Meet Jesus?

It may be that some nominal Christian has read this book, some church member who is not sure he has ever been saved. Perhaps some casual reader has picked up this book who has never claimed to be a child of God and who has never been born again. If so, I beg you in Jesus' name, get ready, get ready, for Jesus is coming! The foolish virgins went out to meet the Bridegroom with no oil, and the door was shut in their faces. Their lamps went out.

Nothing will take the place of the oil of salvation, and I urge you today to put your trust in Jesus. You are a sinner. Your sins have brought condemnation upon you and the greatest of all sins is that you have not trusted in Jesus as your Saviour. John 3:18 says: "He that believeth on him is not condemned: but he that believeth not is condemned already, because he hath not believed in the name of the only begotten Son of God." If you have not trusted Jesus, then you are guilty of the same kind of sin as will be the Man of Sin, the Antichrist. The ruin that will come on the Man of Sin may be yours too, for if Jesus comes today and you are unsaved, you will be left behind to go into the reign of the Man of Sin and the Great Tribulation on this earth.

If you are left here when the Christian people are taken away, you are likely to commit the unpardonable sin. Multitudes will, for every one whose name is not written in the book of life will take the mark of the beast, the Man of Sin; and when one does, he will be forever lost with no chance to escape. When mother and sister and wife are taken away, when every true church is closed, and when every saved person is gone, what will you do? Some will be saved, but many, many more will not.

And if you miss the rapture, you miss the wedding feast in Heaven. Then, suppose you should be saved in the Great Tribulation, you would be marked for destruction, for persecution, and torture and death. For the Bible teaches that those who will not take the mark of the Antichrist will not be allowed to buy nor sell, will not be allowed to make an honest living, and will be hunted and hounded and must hide themselves in the caves and mountains because of the persecution. There is everything to lose if you are not ready when Jesus comes.

And the most likely thing is that you will lose your soul. It is wicked to delay. The Scriptures say: "Today if ye will hear his voice, harden not your hearts." Now is God's time. You can be saved right now if you will in your heart put your trust in Jesus. I hope you will. Nothing can make you ready for the coming of Jesus—not baptism, nor church membership nor moral integrity —no, nothing but being born again, born of the Spirit, becoming a child of God. And you can have that new birth today if you simply trust in Jesus Christ as your Saviour, depending on Him with all your heart. He loves you, and He died for you. Trust Him for salvation and be ready for the coming of Christ.

"Even So, Come, Lord Jesus!"

When Handel had finished his oratorio, "The Messiah," and the glorious climax of the Hallelujah Chorus rang in his mind and heart and ears, he was transported with joy, and almost he could see the glorious coming of the Lord Jesus Christ.

I remember when after five years of toil I completed preparation of a correspondence course on the whole Bible with my lessons on the Book of Revelation. As I dictated the comments on the last two chapters I was so exalted and so thrilled I walked up and down in my study as I dictated. Tears ran down my face, and my voice trembled as I realized a little of the marvel of the glorious rapture of Christians.

What must have been the feeling of the beloved John when on the Isle of Patmos he wrote down the words that were given to him by Jesus Christ? The book of Revelation tells us of the coming revelation of Jesus Christ to all the nations of the earth. John wrote down the plagues that would come on this earth. He wrote down the glorious return and the rapture of Christians. He wrote down that august scene of the twentieth chapter when he said, "And I saw the dead, small and great, stand before God!" And then he tells us how the New Jerusalem is to come down out of Heaven to a new earth surrounded by new heavens, and how God the Father and the Son are to be forever on this glorious paradise that needs no sun, for they are the light of it, and needs no temple, for they are the temple! He tells us how God shall wipe away all tears from our eyes, and how there shall be no more death nor pain nor sorrow, for the former things are passed away. And then the exultant John, on the highest mountain peak of divine inspiration ever given to mortal man, tells us, "And the Spirit and the bride say, Come. And let him that heareth say, Come. And let him that is athirst come. And whosoever will, let him take the water of life freely" (Rev. 22:17). Then John writes down the solemn warning from God that no man is to take from or add to the words of this prophecy. And then he tells us how the Lord Jesus said, "Surely I come quickly."

And finally when the words of Jesus rang out, "SURELY I COME QUICKLY," John answered back with all the inspired passion of his soul, "Amen! Even so, come, Lord Jesus!"

So my heart cries it today. Come, Lord Jesus, come! The drought of a seared and parched land calls for You! The hatred and bloodshed and disappointment and terror of war call for You! The hungry hearts of Your children bleed! The whole world groans in travail! This earth which was once the paradise of God longs to be made whole! The desert should blossom like the rose! Instead of the thorns should come up the fir tree! From Jerusalem should go out the law! Thy saints should reign with Thee! The meek should inherit the earth! Wrong, now reigning, should be put down! Come, Lord Jesus, come! Come! Amen!

Inspirational!
Convicting!
Practical!

742 HEART-WARMING POEMS

Compiled. Contains many of Dr. Rice's own poems along with those by the best Christian and classical poets such as Shakespeare, Wordsworth, Tennyson, Crosby, Flint, Havergal, and others. Other contemporary writers are Bill Harvey and L. O. Engelmann. Poems are grouped under different topics; also carefully indexed as to authors, titles and first lines. 333 large pages. **$6.95**

"DO RIGHT!"

By the late Dr. Bob Jones, Sr. A rich, spiritual legacy has been left by this "giant of the faith" in this volume of 16 of his best messages. Note some of the chapter titles: "Do Right Though the Stars Fall," " 'Rabbit Chasers,' " "Leaving All for Jesus," "Cooperating for Soul Winning," "Lot, the Compromiser," and "Where Are We Headed?" Every preacher and ministerial student should ponder these sermons. 317 pages. **$6.95**

THE HYLES SUNDAY SCHOOL MANUAL

By Dr. Jack Hyles. This is Volume II in the Hyles Manual Series. A comprehensive blueprint for building a large soul-winning Sunday school, combining the wisdom of the sages from the Sacred Pages with tried-and-proven methods of a modern-day, eminently successful Sunday school staff and organization, the First Baptist Church Sunday School of Hammond, Indiana. Another large volume, 256 pages. **$5.95**

Postal Rates: Up to $2—70¢; up to $5—90¢; over $5—15%. Tenn. residents please add 6% Sales Tax.

SWORD OF THE LORD   Murfreesboro, Tennessee 37130

Intensely Interesting Books!

Two Dogs and Peace of Mind

By Dr. Lee Roberson, famed pastor of Highland Park Baptist Church, Chattanooga, Tennessee. In addition to the striking sermon title from which the book gets its name, there are 10 other challenging messages in this slick-covered, attractively illustrated volume of 115 pages. Some others are: "Shouting Stones," "Somebody's Grandfather," "Roses in December," "The Key to Victory," and "The Sensation of Death." Homiletical, illustrated, scriptural messages. Good model preaching.

$1.95

With Miss Viola Through Bible Lands

An up-dated, revised, enlarged edition of a warmly received and reviewed devotional travelogue by Dr. John R. Rice's gifted personal secretary, Dr. Viola Walden. Dr. Walden has taken so many trips to the Holy Land and related countries that she finds it difficult to remember just how many times she has gone, but always it has been in the capacity of assistant director of Sword Tours with Dr. Rice. These experiences, together with continuous diligent study, constitute her a recognized authority. The book is illuminating, refreshing and spiritually as well as factually instructive. 21 chapters, over 200 pictures, maps and drawings. 253 extra-large pages.

$5.95

Sword Scrapbook No. 2

Compiled by Dr. Viola Walden, with editorial counsel from Dr. John R. Rice. A literary paradise for preachers, MCers, lecturers, church paper editors, writers, etc. Prose, poetry, anecdotes, sermonettes—some serious, some humorous, others patriotic, devotional, spiritual, evangelistic. Contains an exhaustive classified index; big 8½" x 11" multi-colored pages—a most attractive gift item for any occasion! Elegantly clothbound with matching dust jacket. 233 pages,

$6.95

POWER *and* BLESSING

THE POWER OF PENTECOST

$5.95

. . .the Fulness of the Spirit, by Dr. John R. Rice. When Jesus, in John 7:37-39, invited, "If any man thirst, let him come unto me, and drink," the context explains that the "living water" of which He spoke was clearly the Holy Spirit in the life of the believer. This large volume is devoted to a detailed, thoroughly scriptural explanation of just about everything taught in the Bible on the Holy Spirit. It will not only refresh your soul, but through you, the lives of others about you. 15 chapters, 441 pages.

CHRIST IN THE OLD TESTAMENT

$4.50

By Dr. John R. Rice. Even a Campbellite preacher, after carefully ''and .honestly reading through this scholarly volume, would have to conclude that the Old Testament has much more than a mere historical and research value to the Christian of today, but that rather it is every bit as much the inspired Word of God, exalting the life, ministry, death, resurrection, and coming again of Christ as fully as does the New Testament. Contains 6 major divisions, 26 chapters.

Postal Rates: Up to $2—70¢; up to $5—90¢; over $5—15%. Tenn. residents please add 6% Sales Tax.

SWORD OF THE LORD   Murfreesboro, Tennessee 37130

7 Great Commentaries—All by Dr. John R. Rice

Church of God at Corinth (Commentary on I and II Corinthians) by Dr. Rice. Surprisingly up-to-date, practical, down-to-earth teaching on local church problems. 29 chapters, 271 pages, **$6.95**

Filled With the Spirit (Commentary on Acts)—A verse-by-verse teaching on the Holy Spirit: New Testament churches, their message and method; speaking with tongues; dispensational truth; and soul winning. 28 chapters, 55 pages, **$6.95**

King of the Jews—A verse-by-verse commentary on Matthew reflecting the scholarly diligence and discipline of an editor. Profound yet simple. A best seller. 28 chapters, 555 pages, **$6.95**

Son of Man (Commentary on Luke)—Profundity clothed in simplicity in this volume of verse-by-verse Bible teaching. 24 chapters, 563 pages, **$6.95**

Son of God (Commentary on John)—Same attractive features as other commentaries, PLUS being profusely illustrated with pictures throughout. 21 chapters, 416 pages, **$6.95**

"In the Beginning. . ." (Commentary on Genesis), Excellent help on Creation, the Flood, "Gap" Theory, Evolution, etc. Another great verse-by-verse commentary. 559 pages, **$6.95**

"Behold, He Cometh!" Verse-by-verse commentary on the Book of Revelation. Allegedly mysterious Scripture made plain and practical. Complete text of Scripture included with lucid comments. 22 chapters, 348 pages, **$6.95**

Postal Rates: Up to $2—70¢; up to $5—90¢; over $5—15%. Tenn. residents please add 6% Sales Tax.

SWORD OF THE LORD   Murfreesboro, Tennessee 37130